ACTOR-
MUSICIANSHIP

ACTOR-
MUSICIANSHIP

JEREMY HARRISON

FOREWORD BY
JOHN DOYLE

Bloomsbury Methuen Drama
An imprint of Bloomsbury Publishing Plc

B L O O M S B U R Y
LONDON · OXFORD · NEW YORK · NEW DELHI · SYDNEY

Bloomsbury Methuen Drama

An imprint of Bloomsbury Publishing Plc

Imprint previously known as Methuen Drama

50 Bedford Square	1385 Broadway
London	New York
WC1B 3DP	NY 10018
UK	USA

www.bloomsbury.com

BLOOMSBURY, METHUEN DRAMA and the Diana logo are trademarks of Bloomsbury Publishing Plc

First published 2016

British Library Cataloguing-in-Publication Data
A catalogue record for this book is available from the British Library

ISBN: PB: 978-1-4725-0963-5
ePDF: 978-1-4725-1377-9
ePub:978-1-4725-1457-8

Library of Congress Cataloging-in-Publication Data
A catalog record for this book is available from the Library of Congress

Typeset by Fakenham Prepress Solutions, Fakenham, Norfolk NR21 8NN
Printed and bound in India

Dedicated to K, J and M

CONTENTS

FOREWORD

How exciting that, at long last, a serious and excellent book has been written about actor-musicianship. It is thrilling for those of us who have been around for a long time to see that this wonderful storytelling method has become an accepted and ever-developing means of making theatre. Jeremy Harrison has been a major player in the journey of this work and there is no more appropriate person to write the first text exploring how it started, how it developed and where it is going.

Actor-musicianship has been around for centuries, but it was only in the latter part of the last century that it was given a name, formalized as a technique and even taught in colleges. It has grown from being explored by a few artists in a few theatres in the United Kingdom to being a language that is used in many countries by many differing and individual artists. I myself use this theatrical language in the United States where I also teach the subject at Princeton University. Who ever knew that so much could happen so quickly?

This book is not only an excellent teaching tool, but also a fascinating study for all those interested in how theatre is developing in the twenty-first century. It has been a great journey for all of us who have participated in the development and I am sure that every reader will find the journey captured through this book fascinating and enlightening. Actor-musician work brings great joy to both performer and viewer. I am confident that this book will bring the reader equal joy and fascination.

John Doyle

INTRODUCTION

This is the story of an alternative theatre movement: of back-of-a-van tours and Broadway opening nights, of performances under canvas and in the glittering light of London's West End, of working on instinct and raw talent, of determination and passion. It is the story of the creative soul's fight to express itself in whatever way it can, indeed in every way it can. It is the dreamer's story, the non-conformists', the champion-of-new-audiences'. It is the story of the 'f**k it!'[1] school of theatre making, that opens towards its spectators, that invites and includes. The story of the rough, the poor, the theatrical.[2] It is the story of Dionysus and Apollo,[3] of an ethos and a culture, perhaps even a subculture, that has emerged blinking into the mainstream. In many ways it mirrors the story of theatre itself; the actor-musician has after all been with us since its emergence, if such an emergence can be traced to a single moment. He was present in the rituals of the drummer-storyteller,[4] and the chanting and music-making of the Greek Chorus. Actor-musicians can be found throughout Western theatre history: from the musicality woven into Shakespeare's plays,[5] to the rousing ballads of Bertolt Brecht[6]. It is also deeply woven into my own story. I grew up with a passion for music and theatre and with very little formal musical training I found my way to learning some fourteen instruments by ear, leaving London's Royal Academy of Dramatic Art in 1987 just as actor-musicianship was exploding into mainstream theatre across the UK. My career as an actor-musician tracked much of the recent history of the movement and saw me working with many of its leading exponents including Bob Carlton,

John Doyle, Peter Rowe, Sarah Travis, Greg Palmer and Catherine Jayes. I now run Rose Bruford College's Actor Musicianship training programme, which sees a steady stream of graduates in a range of disciplines continuing to develop this most interdisciplinary and collaborative of theatre practices. Rose Bruford College Directing graduates now produce actor-musician shows across the UK and in Europe and its actor-musician performers can be seen in a wide variety of shows from children's theatre to mainstream musicals. Sam Palladio has even taken his actor-musician training into his starring role in HBO's hit TV series *Nashville*. Actor-musicianship shows no sign of slowing down, with employment rates and agent take-up soaring in the UK and more and more theatres and drama schools turning on to its visceral, theatrical appeal. American audiences have embraced the form and one of its leading exponents, John Doyle, now spends most of his time there, including as a visiting professor at Princeton.

Actor-musicianship has become a feature of the theatre landscape on both sides of the Atlantic: the right time then for a book that explores its history and approaches to working with this very particular brand of multi-skilled actor. What follows are a series of chapters that aim to define the practice of actor-musicianship and examine how it can be developed by performers, directors, musical directors, designers and theatre makers. I have attempted to draw on theoretical perspectives to support the discussion where appropriate, but in the main this book is a record of theatre practice as it is and has been employed by those who have been responsible for the development of this unique theatre art form, locating it as a development that has its starting point in British theatre culture, but with a precedent in other countries including America.

Let us begin with actor-musicianship's journey from the UK populist theatre movement of the 1950s and 1960s, through to its award-winning presence in the musical theatre mainstream.

Notes

1 The term 'f**k it' was used in an interview with Paddy Cunneen conducted for this publication on 12 September 2014, but it also reflects the spirit invoked by many contributors to the book and indeed in actor-musician rehearsal rooms to this day. The phrase captures the sense of acceptance that this is a hybrid form and that the performers need to be empowered to try things that they may not get right straight away. It is in many ways the practitioner's way of breaking the stranglehold of specialism that can limit this sort of interdisciplinary work.

2 The inference here is to Grotowski's notion of a 'poor theatre', as articulated in his book *Towards A Poor Theatre*, which has received several English translations including one edited by Eugenio Barba (London: Routledge 2002); and Peter Brook's notion of 'rough theatre' as articulated in *The Empty Space* (first pub. MacGibbon and Kee 1968).

3 In *The Birth of Tragedy: Out of the Spirit of Music* Friedrich Nietzsche writes about how tragedy and by extension other art works have power over us because of the way they blend the Dionysian with the Apollonian. In music, he suggests, we find this marriage of the instinctive and the intellectual and only when the two forces are harnessed does art truly enable catharsis in the human soul.

4 John Blacking's work with the Venda tribes of South Africa is just one reminder of the importance of the making of music within ritual storytelling and tribal practice; his studies of their music and music-making can be found in much of his writing including his seminal book *How Musical is Man* (Washington, DC: University of Washington Press 1972). The connection between music and the transmission of cultural knowledge, throughout performative music-making and song, can be found throughout the work of ethnomusicologists.

5 Shakespeare's plays are littered with examples of integrated music-making, from Feste's songs in *Twelfth Night*, through to examples of musicians entering scenes, such as in *Cymbeline* Act 2, Scene 3. In some versions of the text, including the quarto of 1603, it is also suggested that Ophelia enters playing the lute in Act 5, Scene 4. From the wills of actors in the company, such as Augustine Phillip's *Last Will and Testament of 1605*, we know that many of his actors were also musicians, a fact reflected in Chapter 7 of Lois Potter's *The Life of William Shakespeare: A Critical Biography* (Hoboken,

NJ: Wiley-Blackwell 2012), where Augustine and Kemp are cited as examples of actors who were also musicians.

6   Brecht's instructions on the use of music in Epic Theatre includes a suggestion that musicians should not be hidden. This is explored in *The Threepenny Opera* and other plays, including *Baal*, the story of a poet, whose songs are integrated into the work, suggesting the role is designed for an actor-musician, a notion supported by the BBC version of 1982, which saw David Bowie as the wastrel Baal, accompanying himself on a battered, banjo-like instrument. A record of his performance is at present still available on YouTube: http://www.youtube.com/watch?v=jnyXoFlyB1Q (accessed 24 September 2014).

1

FROM THE BUBBLE
TO BROADWAY

For audiences enjoying the current popularity of actor-musician work on Broadway and in London's West End,[1] it is hard to imagine the very humble beginnings of the movement, which are of stark contrast to the bright lights and high ticket prices. Actor-musicianship has its roots in the rich and deeply socialist soil of the 'counter-theatre movement'[2] when in 1936 radical theatre maker Joan Littlewood and her then partner Ewan MacColl established Theatre Union, later to be become the influential Theatre Workshop.

The vision for this new venture is perhaps best summed up in Theatre Union's bold manifesto:

> The great theatres of our times have been popular theatres, which reflected the dreams and struggles of the people. We want a theatre with a living language, a theatre which is not afraid of the sound of its own voice and which will comment fiercely on society as did Ben Jonson and Aristophanes and introducing music and dance style of theatre.[3]

This correlation between a popular theatre and music was central to the company's identity and a tenet both Littlewood and MacColl shared. Implied in the manifesto was a sense that music, and in particular popular music, had become separated from theatre, informed by the gradual emergence of specialism in the processes of theatre making, which gathered momentum after the development of opera. Musicians in theatre were not included within the broader notion of performer but separated, perhaps even elevated. They were regularly placed in orchestra pits either under or off-stage and often required high levels of specialist training, as the technical demands and sophistication of music increased. Audiences as a result developed a set of expectations associated with their presence on stage, which David Roesner suggests involves them being 'mostly invisible, physically insignificant or transparent'.[4] This was a far cry from the theatre of Shakespeare or the Greeks that had embraced the integration of music and music-making, augmenting the presence of musicians with actors who played musical instruments. Compared to the developments in America, the British Musical Theatre lacked the visceral impact and directness offered by the folk club; neither did it have the weight or ambition to speak to the 'dreams and struggles' of Littlewood and MacColl's working-class audience. Instead it was the theatre of the Renaissance and of Ancient Greece on which Theatre Union's vision was modelled. Ewan McColl, then known as Jimmie Miller, spoke of the type of actor that he and Littlewood were seeking to recruit:

> We said the actors in our theatre must be able to dance, to sing, to play musical instruments, to do acrobatics and to act in a perfectly formal way, and it was alright saying this, but we didn't know how to bring it about. It's one thing to have a desire, but another thing to carry that desire into practice.[5]

MacColl, who was steeped in the British folk tradition, understood the theatrical power of music, its ability to tell a story and hold its audience. His ideas enriched and informed Littlewood's, who developed a way of working and an aesthetic that was to influence broader theatre culture immeasurably, as the company changed its name to Theatre Workshop and moved into the then run-down Theatre Royal Stratford East, in a predominantly working class area of East London. This heady mix of music and politics was to be embodied in what was to become the company's best-known piece.

Oh, What a Lovely War! premiered in Stratford in March of 1963 and 'remains an extraordinarily forward-looking fusion of popular entertainment and militant propaganda',[6] an irreverent blend of stirring Music Hall songs, physical theatre and politics. Although it has been given several actor-musician reworkings since 1963[7], the original production saw the acting company accompanied by a dedicated band of specialist musicians, although absorbed into the style of the show. MacColl's ambition to use multi-skilled actors to play the instruments seems to have indeed been too difficult a desire to put into practice at that stage.

The integration of music and music-making also fascinated John Arden, another fiercely political playwright at the height of his powers in the same London of the late 1950s and 1960s. He too sought for a dynamic and new theatre form that embraced what he called 'the ballad tradition'.[8] Throughout his writing career he strove, first alone and then with his wife and writing partner Margaretta D'Arcy, to find ways of integrating the power of music and musicians into his writing and performance aesthetic. *Serjeant Musgrave's Dance*, which premiered in 1959 at the Royal Court Theatre, is perhaps his most enduring work. The play blends a mix of song, lyric poetry and heightened dialogue in a bold theatrical style, and although the production did not include actors who played instruments[9] it could be seen as a move against the ideas of specialism and separation and towards a notion of 'total theatre', which was a term coined to describe work that blended music, movement and text, used particularly in connection with the National Theatre's 1964 production of Peter Shaffer's *The Royal Hunt of the Sun*, which came to Broadway the following year.

It was in this cultural climate that a young female actor and director was working in the North of England for an eclectic audience in schools, community centres and working men's clubs. Based at Sheffield Playhouse, Glen Walford formed her alternative to the main house company named Theatre Vanguard in 1966. With an instinct for what might meet the needs of her largely working class audience, she, like MacColl, sought to fill her company with multi-skilled actors, in an attempt to create something 'more merry and inclusive'.[10] The company, which included a young Alun Armstrong, would devise and write new work that integrated the making of music, in a style that embraced cabaret. By 1970 she was freelancing as a director at Liverpool's Everyman Theatre, a name which was later to become synonymous with actor-musicianship, then Nottingham Playhouse, Edinburgh's Traverse Theatre and London's Royal Court. It was while she was at the Court that she was invited to create a mobile theatre by the Greater London Arts Association, in an attempt to reach out to new audiences in the capital, and so with a nod towards the circus and all the theatricality and artistic breadth that entailed, a reluctant Walford founded The Bubble Theatre in 1972.

The company performed in a tent or 'plastic bubble' as she conceived it, that floated between local parks and heathland, finding new audiences in London's often deprived outer boroughs. Basing its artistic policy on the ideas established in Theatre Vanguard and with Littlewood's populist theatre model in mind, Walford duly put out a call for actors who played musical instruments for her inaugural tour of a new piece to be called *The Blitz Show*. In common with *Oh, What a Lovely War!* this opening gambit for the newly formed company was conceived not as a frivolous knees-up, but as a fiercely political piece. The cast included playwright Shane Connaughton, who at his audition, in the words of Glen Walford, 'diddley-dooed on a range of instruments and pretended to balance six bicycles on his nose'. There was no 'fancy instrumentation', just a use of what was to hand. Many of the first company members played guitar, which had proved so useful in earlier Theatre Vanguard work because of its portability and association with both rock'n'roll and folk music. This same use of guitar playing actors had become part of the aesthetic of the Theatre in Education movement that was beginning to establish in theatres like Coventry's Belgrade and that Walford had drawn on in her own work in Sheffield schools.

The show was well received. Michael Coveney wrote in the *Financial Times* of how the company had avoided the pitfalls of 'pretentiousness and over-statement'[11] that so often characterized theatre taken to the masses. The presence of actor-musicians was key to achieving this sense of simplicity and connection, a fact the show's information leaflet reflected:

> At least two of the six (cast) should be fairly experienced musicians; these were guitarists in the Bubble production, but could be pianists, banjo players etc … One should guard against the over-lavish however. All should be able to sing reasonably well … *The Blitz Show* was staged in the round, with an audience of no more than 100, and this intimacy was reinforced by the friendliness of the actors, who broke down normal reserves between audience and performers.[12]

For Walford the show also broke down social barriers, appealing to working-class and middle-class audiences alike. The integration of music-making was part of this broad appeal, not only reflecting the informality and energy of the pub band and working men's club, but also tapping into the aesthetic and tone of the counter-theatre movement. Throughout the late 1960s and early 1970s companies such as women's groups Siren and Sadista Sisters were integrating music-making into their work, developing a style of theatre heavily influenced by the aesthetic of the rock and pop gig. London-based political theatre company Belt and Braces, formed off the back of 7:84 England in 1973, would also use this idea in their shows under the umbrella *The Belt and Braces Roadshow*.[13] The Bubble was part of what might be seen as a theatre revolution, caught up in the coat tails of the 1960s and informed by Littlewood's Theatre Workshop. It was a movement away from elitism in all its forms. Not unlike the later Punk bands, these early actor-musicians celebrated the power of the three-chord trick, levelling the playing field for both performers and audience. As Bob Carlton later reflected:

> The Bubble was an almost evangelical organization that took a tent out, pitched it on someone's football pitch and did theatre. The real

motivation behind actor-musician work was that if you were the sort of person that doesn't go to the theatre, you see someone giving a performance of Hamlet and you think, 'Yeah, but if I could remember the words and I had the bottle to stand there, I could do that'. Someone plays three chords on an acoustic guitar at the same time and they go, 'Good God! A musician!' and the respect is different … it was about winning your spurs.[14]

The integration of music-making and the use of multi-skilled performers became something of a hallmark for Walford's theatre-in-a-bubble, cementing its identity as one of the new wave of alternative, left-wing theatre companies in London, uniting audiences in deprived Hackney council estates with the more affluent residents of boroughs such as Sutton, all encompassed by the company's mission to bring theatre to the capital's masses.

As a development of this artistic policy, Ian Milne, an early company member, began creating regular evening shows, which he called *The Bubble Band Show*.[15] Like *The Blitz Show*, these performances were framed as a music gig and included a range of material such as songs and sketches. A version of *The Beggar's Opera* reviewed by *The Stage* in 1977 also included musicians who would 'leave their stands to take part in the action'.[16]

Forbidden planets

The use of actor-musicians at the Bubble continued throughout the 1970s, when artistic directorship passed to Bob Carlton.[17] Carlton, under Walford's mentorship, picked up this baton and developed the concept in a series of productions including Shakespeare's *The Taming of the Shrew* and Brecht's *Happy End*.[18] In *Happy End*, which included a mixed cast of musicians and actors who played instruments, he encountered a problem: while the actors could move away from their music, the musicians were reluctant to learn their parts, as this would limit their ability to bring in deps. This frustrated Carlton[19] who made a decision to cast only actor-musicians in his next season, freeing him to take the idea of the band show to new heights.

Kate Edgar, Musical Director and company member from 1981, who studied alongside Bob at Hull University, recalls how the first of these shows was conceived:

> I remember going to a Bubble event in 1980. Glen had organized this show and I always remember Brenda Blethyn, who was a member of the Bubble in those days, doing some trick where she balanced a pint of beer on her head. There was a lot of loyalty and a lot of music and a lot of people playing instruments ... but what Bob did was to develop this band show idea ... I remember him ringing me one Saturday morning and telling me he had had a really good idea for the late night show, that he wanted to base around the Scottish Play and would I come round to talk about it. I remember getting on the tube and going to the East End ... . We walked into Bob's local pub and there was a naff pub singer performing, and as we walked in this guy sang *From A Jack to a King*.[20] We both looked at each other and said, "Well there you are, that's your show." And then Bob went off and wrote it.[21]

For Carlton the experience was pivotal, a reminder of how one song can encompass an entire narrative. The title alone encapsulated the essence of the *Macbeth* story and enabled him to begin the process of conceiving of a theatre show that incorporated a band within its dramaturgical framework. The result was *The Hubble Bubble Band Show*, the precursor to the later *From A Jack to a King*, first performed as a late night band show at the Bubble in 1982. It moved away from the fragmentary, cabaret shape, by setting the story in the heart of the band itself: Terry King, a rock'n'roll star and lead singer is brutally murdered by the band's drummer Eric Glamis, encouraged by his girlfriend, the beautiful singer Queenie. Eric then becomes the front man, only to be haunted by the ghost of King at his debut gig. The show used cod Shakespeare as its text and was peppered with songs from the rock'n'roll stable, which shaped and helped tell the story: *Shaking All Over* was the song the terrified Glamis sings at his fateful debut gig and *So You Wanna Be A Rock'n'Roll Star* the song taught to him by Queenie; the final acceptance of his new-found status crowned by a sparkling guitar solo, delivered by actor-musician Matt Devitt, a hugely gifted and swift-fingered guitarist who joined the Bubble direct from the civil service, in response to one of Carlton's casting calls. The show was such a success that the Bubble's board commissioned a full-length piece for the following season using the same format. This time, with *The Tempest* as its source, Bob created the show that was to change his fortunes and those of the actor-musician movement forever: *Return to the Forbidden Planet.*

Planet, as the show became affectionately known by fans and actor-muscians, was first performed in 1983 as part of the Bubble's summer season. Like *The Hubble Bubble Band Show* it blended quick-fire Shakespearean parody with the best of rock'n'roll, but added a stylish twist with its nod toward 1950s Americana, inspired by the cult film *Forbidden Planet*,[22] which was itself a take on *The Tempest.* Dressed in his space suit Captain Tempest opened the show with the call 'Friends, Crewmen, Passengers lend me your ears',[23] inviting us to join his Scientific Survey Flight and to enter a world of hairdryer ray-guns and guitar toting crew, complete with its own saxophone-playing, roller-skating robot. To the driving drum intro of *Wipe Out*,[24] the Bubble's band show had taken off.

Planet was a more assured and inventive piece, the band was still present, but this time it formed the structure of the spaceship and though incidental to the narrative, it was central to the show's performance style. Drawing inspiration from the popular TV series *Star Trek*, the Navigation Officer played by Kate Edgar, the show's MD, was stationed behind a keyboard, made to look like part of the ship's instrument panel. Rodney Ford's design was a blend of the Starship Enterprise and a rock concert. It used the presentational semi-circular shape of the *Star Trek* bridge to create a band-like line-up complete with drum kit and microphone stands. Carlton's playful staging utilized hand-held microphones and all the posturing of a rock'n'roll show, complete with blistering guitar solos from resident guitar hero Devitt, now playing the lovesick Cookie, the ship's cook who has fallen Caliban-like for the beautiful Miranda, daughter of Captain Tempest, marooned on the planet D'Illyria. Cast members were encouraged to play a range of instruments by Edgar, often switching during numbers; guitars were played by two actors at a time, one performing the left hand fingering, the other strumming out the rhythm without missing a beat; all part of the circus of the event, under the Bubble's very own big top. For Carlton it was a means of uniting his love of rock music with theatre, while holding on to his roots as a working-class lad from Coventry. Although gaining a drama degree from Hull University, Bob's heritage remained an important part of his identity. He wanted to make theatre 'that his mum and dad would have wanted to go and see'[25] and it was this marriage of high and low culture that could be found, once again, at the heart of the actor-musician endeavour.

Bob recalls a moment during his time at the Bubble, when he discovered a couple of skinheads messing around outside the tent during a performance. He quickly offered them a free seat inside, in the hope that it would stop them creating a disturbance. When asked what they thought of the show they enthusiastically replied: 'It was great, but when is the theatre going to start?' For Carlton this subverting of the perceptions of theatre was part of the vision and the employing of a repertory company made up entirely of actor-musicians, the way to achieve it. Interestingly it has remained Carlton's modus operandi throughout his career to date. His tenure at The Queen's Theatre, Hornchurch, another building set in the heart of an impoverished Outer London borough, was characterized by the establishing of a regular company of actor-musicians he called Cut to the Chase. The company were through-cast from season to season in plays that used their musicianship and straight plays that called only on their acting skills.

Around the same time that *Planet* was taking off in London Glen Walford had taken on the artistic directorship of Liverpool's Everyman Theatre. Like the Bubble, the Everyman was formed to attract a younger and more diverse audience than its near neighbour and sister theatre The Liverpool Playhouse. Under the artistic directorship of Alan Dossor they had found success with a formula that incorporated popular music, most notably in John McGrath's social musical *Soft or a Girl Considered.* Following Ken Campbell's anarchic and radical stint at the helm, Walford set about creating a 'new artistic policy in which long-running productions, large-scale musical epics, innovative Shakespeare and actor-musician premieres ... supported smaller-scale innovative in-house productions'.[26] As part of this strategy, and in recognition of its success, she quickly invited Carlton to remount *Planet*, as a replacement for a last minute rescheduling of the 1984 season, this time with Stephen Warbeck taking over from Kate Edgar as Musical Director and Navigation Officer.

The Everyman would take actor-musicianship to its heart and the rock'n'roll format in particular. The theatre continues to programme an annual actor-musician rock'n'roll pantomime to this day, the first, *Wack and the Beanstalk*,[27] following on from the success of *Planet.* Like many regional houses the Everyman was struggling financially as Thatcher's economic policies began to bite. The use of actor-musicians was one solution to the problem of how to stage musical theatre without employing both a company of actors and a separate band. It did, however, come with some expense attached, as Nick Stanley, the theatre's manager, was to discover. *Planet* used a number of instruments including a piano on which a Juno 60 synthesizer, used for the space sounds and special effects, would sit. Stephen Warbeck was not impressed with the quality of the Everyman's piano and spent much of the rehearsal process campaigning for it to be replaced – only to be refused by Stanley. On the closing night of *Planet* Warbeck asked permission for an additional repeat of the closing number, which was duly granted. When the time came, he began a manic piano solo, which developed into a Jerry

Lee Lewis-style affair, including the use of his feet, fists and finally a sledgehammer, taken from the roadworks outside the theatre; by the end of the show the piano was reduced to a wreck and Warbeck had achieved his ambition of getting the theatre the new instrument it and its future actor-musicians deserved.

Return to the Forbidden Planet captured the imagination of the Everyman audiences, which included actor Fred Molina, who was rehearsing *Macbeth* at the neighbouring Playhouse. Molina was friends with Nick Kent, who had just been appointed as Artistic Director of The Tricycle Theatre tucked away in Kilburn in North West London. Only a Bakerloo Line ride away from the West End, the auditorium and popular bar would often see theatre's glitterati rubbing shoulders with a local mix of Jewish and Irish theatregoers. Molina suggested that The Tricycle take a risk on *Planet* and with Carlton now a staff director on TV soap *Brookside*, it was left to Glen Walford to steer the show back into London. It was once again a hit and soon began to attract the attention of producers, such as Olivier Award winning Andre Ptaszynski, who immediately approached MGM, the holders of the rights for the *Forbidden Planet* film, in preparation for a West End transfer. The rights were refused and so for a while at least, its intergalactic journey was stalled.

With Glen Walford at The Everyman taking the form to ever greater heights, with ambitious productions such as an actor-musician reworking of Puccini's *Tosca,* under the musical direction of Paddy Cunneen, and the Bubble Theatre continuing to include actor-musicians in its line up, under the successive leadership of first Bob Eaton[28] then Peter Rowe,[29] actor-musicianship was continuing to develop throughout the late 1980s. A steadily growing pool of actors who could happily turn their hand to music-making, was also starting to establish. Fresh from his stint in television, Bob Carlton was also back in the frame, resurrecting his original Bubble company to form a co-operative they named Rhythm Method Productions. Rhythm Method's first outing was a successful remounting of *The Hubble Bubble Band Show,* now under the title *From A Jack To A King,* the cast including newcomers to the show Christian Roberts and Alison Harding. The production caught the attention of Bob Hamlyn, who was running Coventry's Belgrade Theatre at the time. Coventry, with its failing car manufacturing industry, was shaking from the after-shocks of Thatcher's post-industrial Britain. With its tradition of Theatre in Education and eclectic audience, The Belgrade was a natural home for this populist and cost-effective approach. Tired from a four-week run in Edinburgh, Rhythm Method offered *Planet* instead of *Jack*, and so the show was relaunched. Around the same time MGM were back in touch with Ptaszynski; the rights issue was resolved, and so with amplifiers still humming from its run at the Belgrade, Planet came crashing into the West End to begin its run at the Cambridge Theatre on 18 September 1989.

The show was no overnight success: reviews were mixed and, playing to only 300 a night in what was a barn of a theatre, things were looking bleak. Bob Carlton recalls the turning point:

> The men with suits came and they were going to move a Renaissance one-man show with John Sessions called *Napoleon* into The Cambridge. We had a meeting where Andre [Ptaszynski] said, 'We're going to have to put the notice up', and that Monday Kate was running an understudy call on the stage. Now on the Sunday there was a TV show called *Sunday Sunday* hosted by Gloria Hunniford and Brian Glover, and Heather Cooper gave the show a rave review. On Monday I rang the theatre to talk to Kate to see if the box office had picked up and I couldn't get through. So I rang the Stage Door and asked them to get Kate to ring me when she had finished rehearsing, then I rang BT to say that the phone lines are down at the Cambridge Theatre. About an hour later Kate rang me and said: 'The phone lines aren't down, they're just off the hook and there's a queue down Earlham Street.'

Return to the Forbidden Planet was to run at the Cambridge for four years. More importantly for our story, it was also the shock winner of the 1990 Olivier Award for Best New Musical. Actor-musicianship had arrived: not only did the show beat Cameron Mackintosh's blockbuster *Miss Saigon* and Stephen Schwartz's new offering *The Baker's Wife,* it was also nominated alongside *Buddy,* another show that featured a cast of actor-musicians. From its modest roots the actor-musician show had now grown into a high profile and highly commercial younger brother to the musicals that dominated the West End of the late 1980s and early 1990s.

Post-*Planet* pragmatism: The rise of actor-musicianship and austerity in the arts

If Glen Walford and Joan Littlewood were the Godmothers of actor-musicianship, then Margaret Thatcher has to be credited with a role, perhaps as the Wicked Stepmother. The impact of her government's economic policies and the resulting reduction in public subsidy for the arts had created the necessity that had fed invention, but as Michael Billington argues in his book *The State of the Nation*[30] the presence of the musical as the dominant theatrical force at the time was an illustration of 'Thatcherism in action':[31]

> Where British theatre in previous decades had been famed for its writers, actors and directors, in the 1980s it became identified with its musicals – *Cats*, *Starlight Express*, *Les Miserables*, *The Phantom of the Opera*, *Miss Saigon*. Even the big national companies were seduced into believing that a popular musical was a passport to survival.[32]

If the musical was a financial lifeline, then the cost effectiveness offered by actor-musicianship was doubly attractive to those theatres hit hard by cuts. Producers like Paul Elliot and Bill Kenwright could see that this way of working was both popular and made sound financial sense. Kenwright, who alongside his commercial ventures helped to run The Liverpool Playhouse from 1991–6, used actor-musician shows as a bedrock of the theatre's summer programming. Elliot's *Buddy* was just the start of a steady stream of musicals that told the stories of dead rock stars, for a new breed of theatregoer drawn to the theatre for the chance to see their idols take to the stage once more. Whilst some critics complained, producers like Kenwright defended their vision:

> I make no excuse for presenting these 'rock'n'roll musicals' during the summer at the Playhouse. I passionately believe that the theatre has a right, even a duty, to celebrate every aspect of today's society. The rock'n'roll of the fifties helped enormously to shape that society. Almost overnight, barriers of nationality, language and custom were broken, uniting a generation divided by politics, religion and oceans. One of the greatest thrills of my time at the Playhouse has been to witness the heaving, swaying, clapping, full houses that have greeted these summer productions – at a time when normally our theatre has been closed. Rock'n'roll has filled the houses, filled the coffers, and sent a lot of people home very happy.[33]

Shows during this period included the jukebox musical *Good Rockin' Tonite,* which started at The Playhouse in October 1991 before transferring to London[34], and *Imagine*, a version of Bob Eaton's actor-musician show *Lennon* developed originally for the Everyman, which again went to London following productions at the Playhouse in 1992 and 1994. No rock'n'roll star it seemed was left in peace as a swelling stable of actor-musicians were employed throughout the 1990s in a string of commercial tours, with Jerry Lee Lewis, Roy Orbison and even Elvis[35] given the treatment. You did not even have to have died to take advantage of the trend: Bob Carlton's production of *In the Midnight Hour* starred soul singer Geno Washington and his

Ram Jam Band alongside its cast of actor-musicians. These 'dead rock star shows', as they became known among actor-musicians, did not always contain full companies of actor-musicians. A bit like the shows of the early Bubble, they were performed by mixed casts of actor-singers, actors, musicians and actor-musicians, their identity as actor-musician musicals defined by the centrality of the band as the main dramaturgical and staging device. *Are You Lonesome Tonight*, for example, starred Martin Shaw as a bloated, older Elvis, reliving his glory days in front of a visible backing band that included an actor-musician, who took the role of his younger self.

This blending of musicians and actors began to challenge the mechanisms that governed the employment of performers in the UK. Actors, used to working without deps and for a weekly performance fee, began to look at the musicians working alongside them, who were on Musician Union contracts, with shorter working hours, additional rates for doubling and tripling and porterage fees. A haphazard set of arrangements began to emerge as theatres and producers tried to accommodate this new breed of performer. Theatres like the Bubble paid instrument hire to actor-musicians in the early 1990s, while others such as York Theatre Royal would simply cover maintenance charges. Actor-musicians became adept at making the most of these arrangements, with many benefiting from new bows, overhauls and even replacement instruments. The contracting process was also complicated. Early *Planet* casts had been made to join the Musicians' Union as well as Equity when the show came to London. Gary Yershon recalls the difficulties he and Phyllida Lloyd had when trying to employ actor-musicians for their National Theatre production of *Pericles* in the mid-1990s, finding himself bounced between the Casting Department and the Music Department, in an institutional bureaucracy steeped in the tradition of specialism:

> The difficulties only became apparent at moments of *overlap*: contracted actors worked four-hour sessions whereas contracted musicians worked three-hour sessions, for example. The two

departments, casting and music, were as helpful as they could be, but they were hamstrung to an extent by the contracts they had in place, which in turn had derived from the hard line taken over demarcation by both Equity and the Musicians' Union. In spite of these difficulties, productions such as *Pericles* were helpful by laying the problem open to scrutiny.

Ten years later British Equity developed a specialist contract for actor-musicians working in the West End, although similar conflicts continue in the US.

Actor-musician shows were popping up everywhere in 1990s Britain, as directors who had cut their teeth at the Bubble or the Everyman began to export the vision. Peter Rowe continued to employ full casts of actor-musicians for both his rock'n'roll panto-mimes and later for the ground-breaking musicals at Theatr Clwyd, which toured rural Wales in an extraordinarily well resourced mobile theatre, financed by an electricity company. Stoke-on-Trent's New Victoria Theatre, founded by Peter Cheeseman, added to its long history of new writing with regular new music theatre offerings, often written by Bob Eaton, which utilized actor-musicians. The theatre had championed the use of music, especially folk music in its work, which was often responsive to its local community, but now included bold musical adaptations of operas such as *The Barber of Seville*; Rob Swain, Stage Manager on the 1983 production of *Planet*, was also at Stoke as a director, again casting actor-musicians in much of his work, before going on to export this vision to Harrogate. Christopher Honer, working in Chester, Derby and Manchester Library, David Thacker in Chester, Lancaster and the Young Vic and Andrew Manley of EMMA Theatre Company all put actor-musicianship at the forefront of their work. Han Duijvendak, Associate Director at The Everyman from 1983–7, was also creating actor-musician work first at Lancaster's Dukes Theatre and then for Hatstand Productions, a company he set up with Nick Stanley. Colin Sell, who had created music for the Bubble's 1979 show, *Two Lads from London,* was even starting a prototype actor-musician training course with Sue Colgrave, the then Head of Acting at Rose Bruford College (one of London's leading drama schools) with an eye for the avant-garde and alternative. Perhaps the most significant development, however, was when John Doyle, who took over from Glen Walford as Artistic Director of Liverpool Everyman in 1988, began his forays into actor-musicianship. In his hands the fortunes of actor-musicianship were to change once again, as it completed its journey from Bubble to Broadway.

A Good Night Out: John Doyle and the Scottish Ceilidh tradition

After training as an actor at the Royal Scottish Academy of Music and Drama, John Doyle, who grew up on a housing estate in Inverness, began working as a director in the early 1970s, quickly forming Tie-Up, a theatre company that toured small-scale work across the Highlands and islands of Scotland. Like the Bubble, the company took theatre to hard to reach communities, playing village halls and small theatres from the back of a van.[36] Tie-Up was part of a tradition of working-class theatre identified and championed by John McGrath in his book *A Good Night Out*. McGrath's work for 7:84 Scotland was part of a movement against what he saw as the bourgeois values of mainstream theatre, as with Littlewood's ethos music and music-making were very much a part of what characterized this work, perhaps best illustrated in his landmark production *The Cheviot, the Stag and the Black, Black Oil* which David Edgar described as a 'ceilidh form'[37] of theatre. This notion of the ceilidh is something that Doyle frequently cites in his work, locating his work very much within this Scottish tradition. His early work with Tie-Up, however, was soon to be overshadowed by a move into mainstream theatre as he took over artistic directorship of Worcester's Swan Theatre, before moving to Cheltenham's Everyman, where he built a reputation as a 'safe pair of hands'[38] directing a range of work including extant musicals. When he left for Liverpool to take over from Glen Walford, there was widespread speculation in the local press that the board had appointed him to take the theatre down a similar path, 'in clear contrast to the traditionally experimental Merseyside Everyman'.[39] What Doyle was to do, however, was much closer to his experiences in the Highlands, as he explained shortly after taking over in 1989:

> I think this theatre has always been about risks. Cash is an issue which is always hanging around. There are two schools of thought and one is to say we haven't enough money so we'll cut down on productions and do longer runs – or you can say we will do a lot of work here and prove we're worth having and make damn sure we will become indispensible.[40]

The risk taking began when he created, for the first time in over a decade, an in-house company at the theatre. His opening season was 'nothing less than ambitious',[41] including *The Trojan Women*, a musical adaptation of *Lysistrata*, *'Tis Pity She's A Whore* and the premiere of Solzhenitsyn's *Victory Celebrations*. The rock'n'roll pantomimes remained a feature of his programming, but it was not until his fourth season that Doyle himself attempted an actor-musician piece:

> The board wanted me to do a musical, which I didn't want to do, so I chose one that I thought we couldn't do ... My last show at Cheltenham was *Sweeney Todd* and it was Hal Prince's production, scaled down, like every other production of *Sweeney Todd* that had ever been ... and I remember thinking: well this was fun and good and I loved getting to know the piece and everything, but I wasn't satisfied; I didn't feel that I'd done anything with it that was about me. At that time I didn't know if it was even appropriate to do anything about me, my job was to put shows on. And

so when I went to The Everyman I thought, 'I'm going to go to Liverpool and I'm not going to do any musicals' because I've got to get away from that 'doing a good job putting musicals on that are really copies of someone else's work'; I've got to stop that.[42]

Convinced it would be rejected Doyle chose the ambitious and musically complex *Candide*, by Leonard Bernstein. With only a shoestring budget, he was forced to fall back on the Everyman tradition of using actor-musicians, and so with a cast of 12, he and musical director Catherine Jayes created a production which exploded 'like a hand grenade in a nursery'[43] onto the Everyman stage in June of 1992. Though Glen Walford's earlier production of *Tosca* had seen actor-musicianship pushed to a new level of sophistication, it was Doyle and Jayes' *Candide* that seemed to elevate the form in theatre's consciousness. Colin Sell recalls seeing the production, feeling it represented something of a tipping point. Before that point the mainstay of actor-musicianship had been the rock'n'roll repertoire, material that could be achieved by actors with rudimentary musical skills. In Doyle's *Candide,* however, the musical requirement was so much greater, there was a sense that this simply could not be achieved by actors, and yet 'there they were doing it'.[44] For John Doyle it was a release from traditional models of theatre making, a chance to reinvent and rediscover musical theatre and, more importantly for him, a chance to find his voice within it.

Doyle moved to York's Theatre Royal in 1993 and took actor-musicianship with him. As in Liverpool he recruited a repertory company, now made up predominantly of actor-musicians, who performed a season of work, including extant musical theatre pieces he reinvented for their unique skill set. Stiles and Drew's *Moll Flanders* was given the treatment in 1995, the show's climactic musical centrepiece *Ride* seeing Moll and her highwayman lover Jemmy cavorting on a bed astride a double bass. The production won Doyle, and the company, rave reviews in the regional press and a TMA Award for Best Production of a Musical. Then followed productions of

Cabaret, Sondheim's *Into the Woods* and a new commission of an actor-musician version of *Tom Jones* with music by George Stiles. As the musical demands increased, so the work grew in its impact. Audiences simply could not believe what they were seeing, as Doyle's company played entire scores from memory, without a conductor and while giving performances as leading characters. What had started in part as a response to economic realties, had very quickly turned into an artistic choice, a means of reinvigorating musical theatre and of offering mainstream audiences an experience that had all the visceral appeal of those pioneering rock'n'roll shows.

For all its success with regional audiences, however, and with the Olivier Award triumph of *Planet* now a memory, actor-musicianship was still something of a theatre-backwater in the mid-1990s. For those working in the field it became its own subculture and a rich seam of employment, particularly if you could cross the musical divide between rock'n'roll and the more musically challenging work. Multi-instrumental skills were still in demand, but to work consistently, and not just on the glut of Christmas rock'n'roll pantomimes, actor-musicians had to be able to play at least one instrument to a high standard. Nonetheless, the pool of performers was deepening and with the likes of Karen Mann[45] and the original Bubble crew still working regularly, the casting possibilities were broad. You could now find actor-musicians of all ages and on nearly every instrument. There was also a growing number of theatre makers who were developing ways of working with this new form: Greg Palmer, Catherine Jayes and Kate Edgar were a few of the musical directors who became associated with actor-musicianship in the 1990s along with choreographers such as Fran Jaynes.

When John Doyle, exhausted by running theatres, left York in 1996 to pursue a freelance career, he briefly set up Point Five – a company run by actor-musicians from his time in Liverpool and York. There then followed a rerun of *Moll Flanders* at Salisbury Playhouse, before Jill Fraser invited him to The Watermill to reinvent his actor-musician *Cabaret* for this intimate space, tucked in the rolling Berkshire countryside. It was the Watermill's atmospheric and compact auditorium, coupled with Fraser's flair for artistic risk-taking, that would help steer actor-musicianship out of the backwater and into the mainstream once more.

Cabaret was a runaway hit, filling the charming, but non-air-conditioned Watermill to the rafters during the roasting summer nights of 1997. The Kit Kat Club was brought to vivid life by a cast of actor-musicians led by a squealing MC in the shape of the effervescent Simon Walter, who could be seen by exiting audience members running down the stairs from the dressing rooms, set high in the attic space, and diving semi-naked into the theatre's mill pond, as the spirit of the show seemed to burst into the night air of the still English countryside. It was a perfect marriage that was once again, at least in part, the result of constraint, not this time the inability to afford specialist musicians, for by now Doyle was working this way out of choice, but instead the constraint that limited space and budget placed on the storytelling. The shows had to be reinvented in order to fit. For the actors too the Watermill intensified the notion of the ensemble as they worked and lived in close-quarters, within the grounds of the theatre. Rehearsal days would stretch into nights, the shows seeming to grow organically in the theatre's idyllic garden setting.

In the years that followed Doyle returned to the Watermill Theatre each summer creating a sell-out string of compact reworkings of musicals such as *Irma La Douce, Fiddler on the Roof* and *Piaf.* A bold retelling of Bizet's *Carmen* ushered actor-musicianship into the new millennium, followed by a new actor-musician musical by Doyle himself, with music by Sarah Travis, entitled *A Star Danced.* Doyle, Jayes and Travis had become a formidable creative team with *The Gondoliers* transferring to the West End and *Carmen* playing the Royal Opera House's Linbury Studios as part of the 2001 Covent Garden Festival; the diminutive Watermill's remarkable glories were crowned by its 2004 production of *Sweeney Todd,* which was to see Doyle return to the show that had ended both his tenure at Cheltenham and his love-affair with mainstream musicals, this time in a stripped-down and razor-sharp reinvention that he both directed and designed.

Sweeney Todd takes actor-musicianship to the Tonys

John Doyle and musical collaborator Sarah Travis began rehearsals for *Sweeney* in the winter of 2003. With the Watermill's rehearsal space occupied for some of the time, the show was created in a string of makeshift spaces including the fish and chip shop at the Newbury race track. Rebecca Jackson[46] recalls how cold it was, particularly once the company returned to the Watermill's clapboarded rehearsal space, by the kitchen bins at the back of the theatre in January 2004: 'instruments were constantly going out of tune because of the cold and John had to keep telling us off for wearing our coats during rehearsals.'[47] As always with Doyle's processes, however, there was a tangible buzz of creativity in the room and a sense that this was as much a devising process as a rehearsal for an extant musical. By this time the Watermill's actor-musicianship work was guaranteed to sell out and attract national reviews; with one West End transfer under their belts and interest in the 2002 production of *Fiddler on the Roof* only thwarted by an issue with the performance rights, there was a sense of anticipation from all concerned.

The 'stunningly inventive'[48] production opened 4 February 2004 to uniformly strong press notices. Following its seven and a half week run at the Watermill the cast began a short UK tour. It was on the last night of the run, at the intimate Lowry Theatre, that producer Adam Kenwright, son of actor-musician champion Bill, gathered the cast together to tell them that the show was indeed transferring to the West End, finally opening at the Trafalgar Studios in July of the same year.

With actor-musicianship once again enjoying mainstream attention, it was only a matter of time before America would come calling. On a summer's evening in 2004 the call came. John was relaxing at home in Hastings, having just poured a gin and tonic, when the telephone rang. A voice introduced itself as Stephen. Convinced it was an impersonation by one of the cast, Doyle calmly continued, only gradually realizing that it was indeed Stephen Sondheim on the line and that he was not happy. At this stage Doyle was not aware that Sondheim had been sent a video of the London production in order to seek his approval for a Broadway transfer. Doyle's bold reworking had included a cut of the Judge's song, which the publishers had advised was optional. Nonetheless Sondheim was worried and insisted that he came to London to see it for himself. When he eventually saw *Sweeney*, now transferred to the Ambassador's Theatre, he was visibly shaken, not by the alterations, but by the actor-musicians. He loved the show and Sarah Travis' reworking of the musical arrangements, so expertly transposed from full-scale orchestra to an intimate band of accordion, cello, clarinet, violin, guitar and keys:

> When I first wrote this thing all I wanted to do was write a horror story, a Grand Guignol piece … Of all the productions I've seen, this is the one that comes closest to Grand Guignol, closest to what I originally wanted to do. I characterize all the major productions I've seen in terms of a single adjective. Hal's was epic. Declan Donnellan's production was exactly the reverse, it was very intimate. John's, for me, is the most intense … Jonathan Tunick's original orchestrations may be the best ever heard on Broadway, but this is a whole other matter. The variety of sounds she's [Sarah Travis] gotten out of the instruments and also the practical way in which they allow John to work with the performers onstage is extraordinary. But what got me most about the orchestrations is what they did for the play's atmosphere. These are wonderfully weird textures. The sound of an accordion playing with a violin – it's very creepy.[49]

With Sondheim's blessing the show began previews on 3 October 2005 in New York's Eugene O'Neill Theater. Equity restrictions meant that Doyle could only have taken one or two members of the London cast. With such a strong ensemble ethos at the heart of his work, he felt he could not choose one over another and so a completely new American company was created. The producers insisted on a name to lead the company and so alongside Michael Cerveris as Sweeney, Broadway legend and tuba player Patti LuPone was cast as his accomplice, the inventive Mrs Lovett, both joining a company of American actors surprised to discover that for this show a fourth skill was required in addition to the usual triple-threat of singing, acting and dancing.

Actor-musicianship was not new to America. *Buddy* had transfered from London in 1990 running for 225 performances and *Return to the Forbidden Planet* had a 243-show run following its off-Broadway debut at the Variety Arts Theatre in 1991. Sam Mendes' Tony Award winning revival of *Cabaret* came to Broadway in 1998 following a similar treatment at London's Donmar Warehouse. The show, which contained a chorus of actor-musicians, was remounted in New York in 2015. As well as English imports there had been a steady stream of homegrown shows that used music-making as part of their framing such as Connie Ray and Alan Bailey's *Smoke on the Mountain*, which began its life at New Jersey's McCarter Theatre before coming to New York in 1990. Mary Murfitt and Betsy Howie's late 1990s musical *Cowgirls* also used actors who play instruments in the story of a trio of classical musicians booked to save an ailing saloon. Murfitt was a cast member in the 1982 actor-musician show *Pump Boys and Dinettes*, which enjoyed a year-long Broadway run at The Princess Theatre. The creators of *Pump Boys*, guitarist Mark Hardwick and drummer Debra Monk, also wrote *Oil City Symphony* which came to The Circle in the Square in New York in 1987, following productions in Dallas and Baltimore, the story focusing on a group of musicians brought together for a high school reunion concert in memory of their late music teacher. These shows all used music-makers as their conceptual starting point and seemed to draw on the rich seam of variety and cabaret alive in saloons and dinner theatres throughout the United States. Mike Ockrent and Susan Stroman's 1993 Broadway production of Gershwin's *Crazy for You* saw popular variety act The Rhythm Kings embedded into the narrative, providing an actor-musician dimension and a real double bass player for Stroman to animate at the heart of the show's killer dance number *Slap That Bass.* Allan Katz and Eric Frandsen's *Song of Singapore* caused a sensation when it transformed a run-down former Polish Veteran's Hall in Manhattan's Lower Midtown into Freddy's Song of Singapore Café, the venue for a flight of fancy which saw singer Rose of Rangoon transported across the world by a series of songs driven by a band of musicians who were an integral part of the story telling. It had all the hallmarks of actor-musicianship, with integration of instruments and transformation facilitated by both the music and the presence of the musicians themselves. Doyle's *Sweeney*, however, took the idea to a new a level for American audiences. The instruments were not suggested by the narrative, but instead formed the bold conceptual framing now so familiar to UK audiences. With Stephen Sondheim's blessing and six Tony Award nominations, including wins for Doyle and Travis, actor-musicianship had finally been absorbed, at least for the time being, into the fabric of the American musical theatre.

Doyle and Travis' *Sweeney Todd* played for 384 performances in New York before embarking on tours of the United States. Doyle continued his relationship with Sondheim with an actor-musician version of *Company*, which transferred to New York's Ethel Barrymore Theatre in late 2006, following a production instigated by bold producer Edward Stern of Cincinnati Playhouse in the Park. Further US actor-musician productions included a 2010 version of Brecht's *Caucasian Chalk Circle*, at the American Conservatory Theatre in San Francisco, which Doyle directed with original music by composer Nathaniel Stookey. As a Tony Award winning director, John Doyle was able to branch into other work including directing a film and even a version of *Peter Grimes* at New York's Metropolitan Opera. With a visiting professorship at Princeton and a recent appointment as Associate Director of New York's Classic Stage Company, Doyle now spends much of his time in America, bidding farewell to the Watermill Theatre in 2008, with another actor-musician reworking of a Sondheim: *Merrily We Roll Along.* Despite building an infra-structure of actor-musician performers and creatives, such as his American musical director and arranger Mary-Mitchell Campbell, Doyle's work in the States is not exclusively in actor-musicianship. His 2014 production of Rodgers and Hammerstein's *Allegro* for the Classic Stage Company is an exception rather than the rule. Doyle's influence on American theatre practice is still significant, however, with actor-musicianship gradually emerging in the work of other newer companies such as Fiasco, whose founding members Jessie Austrian and Noah Brody were taught by Doyle whilst studying at Rhode Island's Brown University.

A British phenomenon

Actor-musicianship can in many ways be seen as a British phenomenon driven by a set of imperatives – some artistic, some more pragmatic – reflective of the very particular way we have funded and made theatre in this country. It could be viewed as the British take on the American musical theatre form, a position reflected in its presence as a regular feature of the West End and Broadway, in the success of John Doyle's work in the US and in the emergence of actor-musician training courses as adjuncts to existing musical theatre provision in drama schools such as Mountview and Guildford School of Acting, which both have strong profiles as providers of training in musical theatre. Theatres such as the Watermill, currently under the leadership of Rose Bruford graduate Paul Hart, continue to develop actor-musician musicals that both celebrate and subvert the commercial musical form. Nikolai Foster's 2014 reworking of *Calamity Jane* saw an actor-musician cast move from the intimate Watermill stage to national touring in number one venues across the UK, following in the footsteps of Craig Revel Horwood's 2013 actor-musician tour of *Fiddler on the Roof*. These are very much offerings with the mainstream in mind, destined for large houses and hoping for West End and even Broadway transfers. The roots of actor-musicianship in the populist and alternative theatre movement are important to recognize, however, and with that comes the acknowledgement of the influence of European theatre practice, a fact echoed by its long-standing presence on the curriculum of London's Rose Bruford College, which has a tradition of exploring community theatre practice as well as European and mainstream British theatre. Grotowski, Eugenio Barba and Wlodmierz Staniewski all acknowledged the centrality of music and in particular the notion of musicality in their work. Staniewski, in particular, places live music-making at the heart of his company's working methodology and performance aesthetic; Gardzienice are a Polish theatre company who make no distinction between music, text, physicality and voice in their processes and performance and their bold integration of music and song into a visceral blend of physical theatre has been witnessed by audiences around the world. Their influence on theatre makers in the UK and America is not easy to define, but during the research journey for this book Gardzienice and other European companies were cited by British practitioners involved in the development of actor-musicianship. The freedom offered by what might broadly be defined as a European theatre aesthetic certainly inspired John Doyle to develop a more fluid and poetic approach. In rehearsals for the earlier shows at the Watermill and York he would often encourage his actors to consider the European tradition rather than their own model of theatre making, which he regarded as being too bound by text-based linear narrative and psychological realist approaches. Only this broader context, he argued, would enable the inclusion and integration of music-making into the storytelling; interestingly this instruction was often coupled with references to the Scottish ceilidh tradition. Glen Walford also talked of the influence of European work, again as a paradigm that enabled an escape from text as the starting point. Paddy Cunneen cited influences including Dutch theatre company Hauser Orkater,[50] whose very name is a hybrid of orchestra and theatre.

If actor-musicianship offered directors such as John Doyle, Nikolai Foster and Craig Revel Horwood a chance to reinvent musical theatre, then it also provided British theatre makers the chance to break free from the hierarchies implied in theatre making processes governed by the pervading dominance of spoken text. As John McGrath suggests this may be connected to theatre's alignment to middle-class values, which suggest that music in some ways diminishes the intellectual power of plays, even though in much theatre making 'the text may well not be a decisive element'.[51] Placing instruments in the hands of your leading characters challenges notions of how we read and make performance work. In common with the Post Dramatic theatre makers the use of actor-musicians challenges more than just the mode of performance, but as Ewan MacColl acknowledged in the early days of the Theatre Workshop, it also requires new ways of approaching and making theatre. With so little writing for actor-musicians it has been the devising companies that have really embodied this notion. With the high profile successes of companies such as Kneehigh, theatre in the UK and America has seen an upsurge in work that embraces actor-musicianship as part of its performance vocabulary. Even London's National Theatre has embraced this storytelling approach. Tom Morris's *Swallows and Amazons* built on the earlier successes of *Coram Boy* and *War Horse*, including actor-musician elements in its deft retelling of Arthur Ransome's delightful children's story. Actor-musicianship may not always be the primary vehicle, but it is certain that the current theatre zeitgeist very much embraces its interdisciplinary nature. The fringes of theatre are full of young and emerging companies that promote and utilize actor-musicians including Rose Bruford College graduate company Dumbwise[52] and award-winning Fine Chisel,[53] whose show *Dumbstruck* led Musical Theatre Network to develop a new category of award in innovation, for them to win in 2013. Long embraced by the Theatre for Young Audiences sector, there are also countless examples of companies that use actor-musicians including the breathtaking Oily Cart[54] and directors such as Sally Cookson, whose collaborations with composer Benji Blower have led to a number of wonderful shows for children and young people, which place live music-making at the heart of the storytelling.[55] The classical music scene has also spawned a number of musician actor offerings including The Gogmagogs[56] and Sharpwire.[57] Actor-musicians can currently be seen in most regional theatres across the UK and America and in commercial theatres from the West End to Broadway. The Bubble, the Everyman, Stoke's New Victoria, Ipswich's Wolsey Theatre, Theatr Clwyd, the Queen's Theatre Hornchurch and many of the other early champions of the work continue to regularly programme and develop actor-musicianship and have now been joined by a growing number of the major regional theatres across the UK and the USA. The journey from big top to Big Apple may now be complete, but the actor-musician diaspora, it could be argued, is only just beginning to take root.

Notes

1 At the point of writing this chapter there are a number of examples of actor-musician work that have recently played or are currently playing in the West End and on Broadway, including *Once*, *The Commitments*, *The Jersey Boys* and *The Million Dollar Quartet*. In addition there are several touring shows and regional theatre productions in the UK, including The Watermill's tour of *Calamity Jane,* The Ipswich New Wolsey production of *Midsummer Songs* and Coventry Belgrade's production of *Three Minute Heroes*, with John Doyle rehearsing an actor-musician version of Rodgers' and Hammerstein's *Allegro* at the Classic Stage Company in New York, which opened in November 2014.

2 The *Financial Times* offered this description of John McGrath's 1981 book *A Good Night Out:* 'The classic statement of the aims of the counter-theatre movement in this country.' The book includes a description of the work of Joan Littlewood and its influence on theatre of the late twentieth century.

3 Theatre Union's 1936 manifesto as cited in *Joan Littlewood and the People's Theatre*, an *Archive on 4* programme for BBC Radio 4, broadcast on 27 September 2014.

4 Roesner, D., 'Musiking as *mise-en-scene*, Studies in Musical Theatre 4:1', *Studies in Musical Theatre* 4 (1) (August 2010).

5 Ewan MacColl, then Jimmie Miller, interview broadcast as part of *Joan Littlewood and the People's Theatre*, an *Archive on 4*, programme for BBC Radio 4, broadcast on 27 September 2014.

6 *Oh What a Timely Production*, a review of Tim Baker's actor-musician production at Theatr Clwyd in 2003 by Alfred Hickling, published in *The Guardian*, 26 February 2003.

7 There have been a number of productions of *Oh, What a Lovely War!* which have used actor-musician casts, including Tim Baker's production for Theatr Clwyd (ibid.). The rights for the production were granted by Littlewood the day before she died with the caveat that the show was to contain 'no bloody acting', as reported by the director in an interview with Guardian journalist Alfred Hickling entitled *Oh What A Timely Production* (ibid.).

8 Winkler, E. H., *The Function of Song in Contemporary British Drama* (Newark: University of Delaware Press, 1991), 70.

9 Later productions including one by Jeremy Harrison at Rose Bruford College, which was the subject of *Making Musgrave Dance*, an article by Harrison exploring the use of actor-musicianship in performance and process for publication in *Music On Stage* (Cambridge: Cambridge University Press, 2015).

10 Glen Walford in conversation with Jeremy Harrison at her flat in Central London, in an interview conducted for this publication on 18 July 2014.

11 *Financial Times* review 4 May 1972, viewed from Bubblepedia, the archive of the London Bubble: http://www.bubblepedia.co.uk/event/the-blitz-show/ (accessed on 24 September 2014).

12 *The London Blitz Show Information* Bubblepedia: http://www.bubblepedia.co.uk/event/the-blitz-show/ (accessed 24 September 2014).

13 Susan Croft's research into the alternative theatre movement which incorporates Women's Theatre, Gay and Lesbian Theatre, Disabled Theatre and TiE is disseminated in *Unfinished Histories* both as a publication and internet resource: http://www.unfinishedhistories.

com and *Re-Staging Revolutions: Alternative Theatre in Lambeth and Camden 1968–88.* Unfinished Histories and Rose Bruford College 2013.

Susan Croft added the following information in an email to Jeremy Harrison (author) on 2 July 2014:

> I was thinking about your actor-musician research and how many connections there are with the alternative theatre movement and with some of the companies we have documented for Unfinished Histories. A number of companies covered also operated as bands as well as often multi-instrumental singers and musicians while performing in shows including Siren with whom I did a long interview a few years ago (not yet up on the site though there is a large section of it on the Women's Liberation Music Archive web site http:// womensliberationmusicarchive.co.uk/ – we did it jointly), Sadista Sisters (ditto and also on the Unfinished Histories web site), Belt and Braces (a short interview with Gavin Richards but we have a copy of a documentary they made in Sweden with extensive footage of them performing as the band the *Belt and Braces Roadshow* and music played by the actors was integral to all or most of their shows). There is also some material about Foco Novo – I'm thinking in particular about their show *The Ass* with Mike and Kate Westbrook. It also featured Stephen Boxer who is a very accomplished actor-musician. I first saw him years ago in Paine's Plough's *Richard III Part Two* and Paine's Plough in the late 70s/early 80s frequently used actor-musician performers. I think this was also true of a number of Monstrous Regiment shows, especially Brechtian pieces like Vinegar Tom and Scum. Cunning Stunts certainly played instruments as well as performing. Spare Tyre played instruments and performed songs as a key part of their shows. See http://www.unfinishedhistories.com/ history/companies/for pages for all of those except Paine's Plough and Cunning Stunts. There is a particular feminist actor-musicianship of that era in which it was very important to represent women as multi-talented and competent in numerous areas – so they should be seen carrying and erecting the set *and* acting and playing an instrument. Adele Salem talks about some of that in her interview (in relation to the set-carrying etc). Ruth Mackenzie also speaks of it in hers on Moving Parts (see http://www.unfinishedhistories.com/ interviews/interviewees/).

14 Bob Carlton in conversation at an Actor-Musician Forum held as part of the symposium activity at Rose Bruford College in April 2003.

15 Bubblepedia: http://www.bubblepedia.co.uk/event/bubble-
band-show-1977/ (accessed on 30 September 2014).

16 Anne Morley-Priestman reviewing *The Beggar's Opera* for *The Stage*, 31
March 1977.

17 Bob Carlton was Artistic Director of the Bubble from 1979–83.

18 *Happy End* was part of the 1981 Bubble Season. The cast of
actor-musicians included Kate Edgar. Kate went on to become
musical director and collaborator with Bob throughout the 1980s and
1990s.

19 Bob Carlton reflects on this issue both in interviews held with the author
on 26 September 2014 and at an Actor-Musician Forum at Rose
Bruford College in 2003 (see note 22) and in the programme for the
Charity Gala Concert Performance of *Return to the Forbidden Planet*
held on 20 July 2008, available online: http://www.queens-theatre.
co.uk/archive/programmes/Return_to_the_Forbidden_Planet_charity_
gala_2008.pdf (accessed on 30 September 2014).

20 *From A Jack to a King* was a crossover hit for Ned Miller. Its second
release in 1963 topped the country, pop and adult contemporary
Billboard charts in the US, as well as reaching the top five in both the
UK and Ireland. The song was recorded by a number of rock'n'roll
artists throughout the 1960s including Elvis and Jerry Lee Lewis.

21 Kate Edgar in conversation with Jeremy Harrison in an interview for this
publication on 22 September 2014.

22 *Forbidden Planet* was an MGM film released in 1956 starring Walter
Pidgeon, Anne Francis and Leslie Nielsen. Cyril Hume's screenplay,
based on a story by Irving Block and Allen Adler, was a retelling of
Shakespeare's *The Tempest*: a spaceship goes to investigate a long
forgotten planet, only to discover human life and a deadly secret. The
film achieved a cult status amongst sci-fi fans, in part due to its iconic
robot Robby.

23 The opening line from the original 1983 script of *Return to the Forbidden
Planet* that credited Joe Darlinson as writer. Bob Carlton chose the
name of his grandfather as a pseudonym to avoid being accused,
as Artistic Director, of influencing the board of the Bubble who had
commissioned the piece. The first pages of the script can be accessed
via the London Bubble's digital archive: http://www.bubblepedia.co.uk/
event/the-return-to-the-forbidden-planet/ (accessed 25 September
2014).

24 *Wipe Out* is an instrumental song written in the early 1960s by Bob Berryhill, Pat Connelly, Jim Fuller and Ron Wilson. The song begins with a powerful tom-tom riff played on the drum kit. This same riff was used to launch the space flight in *Planet*.

25 Bob Carlton in conversation with the author in an interview conducted for this publication on 26 September 2014.

26 From Glen Walford's biography as published on her website: www.glenwalford.com (accessed 26 September 2014).

27 http://www.everymantheatrearchive.ac.uk/history.htm (accessed 30 September 2014).

28 Bob Eaton was Artistic Director of the Bubble from 1983–5. He had also created shows for The Liverpool Everyman and is perhaps best known for *Lennon*, a musical written with actor-musicians in mind, that explores the story of John Lennon and The Beatles. Bob wrote a number of shows that utilize actor-musicians for The London Bubble, The New Vic, Stoke-on-Trent and Coventry's Belgrade Theatre.

29 Peter Rowe was Artistic Director of the Bubble from 1984–9. He has continued to use actor-musicians throughout his career, including the development of his own rock'n'roll pantomimes, which can currently be seen each Christmas at theatres across the UK including The New Wolsey, Ipswich (where he is Artistic Director), Leeds City Variety and Theatr Clwyd. He also wrote *Midsummer Songs*, with composer Ben Goddard, a new musical for actor-musicians, which premiered at The New Wolsey in September 2014.

30 Billington, M., *State of the Nation: British Theatre since 1945* (London: Faber and Faber, 2007).

31 Billington, M. *Margaret Thatcher casts a long shadow over theatre and the arts. The Guardian*, 8 April 2013.

32 Ibid.

33 Bill Kenwright, programme note from September 1993, cited in R. Merkin, ed., *Liverpool Playhouse*: *a Theatre and its City* (Liverpool: Liverpool University Press, 2012), 197.

34 *Good Rockin' Tonite* opened at The Strand Theatre in January 1992.

35 *Are You Lonesome Tonight?* was Alan Bleasdale's tribute to Elvis Presley that Bill Kenwright launched at The Liverpool Playhouse in 1985, winning Bleasdale The Evening Standard Award for Best Musical. There have been a number of actor-musician musicals featuring Jerry Lee Lewis, including the more recent *Million Dollar Quartet* which was on Broadway, in the West End and national tours of America. *Only the Lonely: the Roy Orbison Story* toured the UK and Europe throughout the 1990s, again a Bill Kenwright production. The show also has a cast recording available through First Night Records.

36 Bridget McCann recalls her time working with TIE-UP in an article for *The Iverness Courier*, 26 September 2009: http://www.inverness-courier.co.uk/Entertainment/Bridget-looks-back-fondly-on-her-apprenticeship-1011.htm (accessed 2 October 2014).

37 David Edgar cited in McGrath, J., *A Good Night Out*, 2nd edn (London: Nick Hern Books, 1996), 33.

38 *Broadway's Other British Hero,* Dominic Cavendish, *The Daily Telegraph*, 20 June 2006: http://www.telegraph.co.uk/culture/theatre/drama/3653260/Broadways-other-British-hero.html (accessed 3 October 2014).

39 Turnbull, O., *Bringing Down the House: The Crisis in Britain's Regional Theatres* (Bristol: Intellect Books, 2009), 176.

40 Ibid., 177.

41 *History of the Everyman: Love at a Loss,* http://www.everymantheatrearchive.ac.uk/history.htm (accessed 2 October 2014).

42 John Doyle in conversation with Jeremy Harrison on 26 March 2014, in an interview conducted for this publication.

43 John Peter, writing in *The Sunday Times* in June 1992, cited in Everyman Theatre Archive, see note 51.

44 Colin Sell, who founded the first training programme for actor-musicians with Sue Colgrave at Rose Bruford College in the early 1990s, in conversation with Jeremy Harrison on 25 September 2014, in an interview conducted for this publication.

45 Canadian actress Karen Mann trained at The Royal Scottish Academy with John Doyle. With the ability to play the trumpet, she soon found herself at the Bubble working with Bob Carlton. Karen went on to specialize in actor-musicianship becoming a regular collaborator on productions by Bob Carlton, Peter Rowe, John Doyle and Craig Revel Horwood. Most notably Karen played Mrs Lovett in Doyle's production of *Sweeney Todd* both at The Watermill Theatre and then in London.

46 Rebecca Jackson, who trained on Rose Bruford College's Community Theatre Arts course, and was taught by staff including Colin Sell, was a regular in John Doyle's shows appearing in *Sweeney Todd*, *Fiddler on* *the Roof, Ten Cents a Dance*, *Merrily We Roll Along* and *A Star Danced,* as well as Christmas shows directed by Doyle, all at The Watermill Theatre. She had also worked on actor-musician shows throughout the 1990s. She played the Beggar Woman in both The Watermill and West End versions of *Sweeney Todd.*

47 Rebecca Jackson in conversation with Jeremy Harrison during an interview conducted for this publication, which took place on 3 October 2014.

48 From Charles Spencer's *Daily Telegraph* review of *Sweeney Todd* at The Watermill Theatre, 4 February 2004.

49 *Cutting 'Sweeney Todd' to the Bone*, Charles Isherwood writing in the *New York Times*, 30 October 2005.

50 Hauser Orkater were a Dutch theatre collective formed by brothers Dick and Rob Hauser in 1972. The name Orkater is a blending of theatre and orchestra and their work always sought to find ways of using live music-making and the band aesthetic as a force which governed both dramaturgy and performance aesthetic. They began creating street theatre and work at music festivals, before moving on to work in theatres and film.

51 McGrath, J., *A Good Night Out,* 2nd edn (London: Nick Hern Books, 1996), 3.

52 Dumbwise was formed in 2008 by John Ward, Eilidh deBonnaire and David Hewson. DeBonnaire and Hewson both trained on Rose Bruford College's Actor Musicianship Programme and Ward on the Directing Programme. They continue to use the shared vocabulary they were exposed to during their training to create original actor-musician shows including an adaptation of Faust and Terry Jones' children novel *Nicobobinus*. Their work regularly tours the UK.

53 Fine Chisel describe themselves on their website as 'a theatre company and a band'. They were formed in 2010 by Tom Spencer and are based in Bristol in the UK. Their work, which includes adaptations of Shakespeare, is often performed in non-theatre spaces, with shows like *Midnight At The Boar's Head* regularly playing pubs. In 2013 they won the MTN Award for Innovation for the Edinburgh run of *Dumbstruck.*

54 Founded over 30 years ago by Tim Webb, Claire de Loon and Max Reinhardt, Oily Cart specializes in work for children under five, and those with complex disability. Their work has toured internationally and they recently advised the Lincoln Centre's Education Department on their approach to making work for children with autism.

55 Sally Cookson is a freelance director based in Bristol. Her collaborations with Bristol-based composer Benji Blower have included the number one tour of *We're Going On A Bear Hunt* and her reworking of *Cinderella* which was seen both in Bristol and then at The Unicorn Theatre in London. Both shows place the music at the heart of the storytelling and include an onstage musician whose performance is integrated into the physical aesthetic and often augmented by music made by members of the cast.

56 The Gogmagogs was founded in 1995 by theatre director Lucy Bailey and violinist Nell Catchpole. Their shows explore how classical string players can use their whole physical presence and personality to create breathtakingly sophisticated musical stories. They have performed at venues including the ICA, Royal Court, Queen Elizabeth Hall and the Bridewell Theatre.

57 Sharpwire is a collaboration between UK cellist, singer and theatre performer Matthew Sharpe and composer Peter M. Wyer. Their one-man operatic thriller *Johnny's Midnight Goggles* was a commission by Tete a Tete and Brighton Festival. The company has since developed into Sharp Productions, which develops integrated performance work that uses classical music as its starting point.

2
JACK AND MASTER

In the previous chapter we explored the history of the actor-musician movement, using key productions to chart its development. In this chapter we focus on the actor-musician as performer. Defining the actor-musician show is not easy: should it be written with actor-musicians in mind? Does the cast need to be made up exclusively of actors who play instruments and if not, then what percentage of the cast needs to have instrumental skill for the definition to apply? A precise set of criteria is difficult to establish. Defining the actor-musician, by comparison, should be a relatively straightforward task: He is an actor who plays a musical instrument; or is she a musician who acts? And there's the rub. This may not seem an important distinction to make, but it is of course crucial to the actor-musician him or herself. It affects how and where they work and what contract is used to employ them, it is central to their identify as a creative artist, which is all ultimately reflective of the pervasive notion of specialism that has shaped the processes and pedagogies that apply to theatre training and production.

The conservatoire movement has a well-established history of specialist vocational training in the distinct disciplines of acting, music and dance. Similarly the infrastructures that have developed to support theatre making have mirrored this siloing effect, from the departmental system of the National Theatre discussed in Chapter 1, to the contracting and employment of actor-musicians, that fell between union agreements with the musicians' unions and actor's

Equity in both the UK and America. It is present in the education system that most performers experience as children, with dance, drama and music again offered as separate curriculum areas taught by specialist teachers, who follow specialist pedagogies, informed by specialist examinations. This is not to say that developing specific skills in isolation is not an important part of creative development, it clearly is, but what of those who possess more than one aptitude and would like to explore the ways in which their various creative outputs can interrelate and co-exist? It seems that the very processes of art making and training have been set up to discourage such inter-disciplinarity, particularly when encapsulated within a single artist. Indeed there is a general suspicion, even mistrust of the idea; as the hackneyed saying warns us, the jack-of-all-trades is, by dint of his very nature, the master of none. But why should this idea carry such pejorative undertones? Is it so bad to be good at more than one thing?

In his book *How Musical is Man?* ethnomusicologist John Blacking challenges Western ideals of music and music-making, setting out an argument based on his research into the Venda people of West Africa:

> If, for example, all members of an African society are able to perform and listen intelligently to their own indigenous music, and if this unwritten music, when analyzed in its social and cultural context, can be shown to have a similar range of effects on people and to be based on intellectual and musical processes that are found in the so-called 'art' music of Europe, we must ask why apparently general musical abilities should be restricted to a chosen few in societies supposed to be culturally more advanced. Does cultural development represent a real advance in human sensitivity and technical ability, or is it chiefly a diversion for elites and a weapon of mass exploitation? Must the majority be made "unmusical" so that a few may become more "musical"?[1]

Blacking's correlation between musical specialism and elitism offers us a potential means of reading actor-musicianship. The act of communicating through music, he implies, is fundamental to the human condition; one only has to look and listen to the world around us to see evidence of this. Music is everywhere from the super-market, to the car radio, our experience of the everyday constantly tempered by its presence. We are all in this sense musical; an inherent musicality informs our everyday engagement with one another and the world around us. Only those who can play an instrument or who have worked professionally in music-making, however, may be called a musician. Even within this distinction we find further layers of hierarchy. To drum your fingers on the table or tap out a rhythm with a teaspoon does not constitute musicianship. The proliferation of jokes about drummers (what do you call someone who hangs around with musicians? – a drummer), are testament to another hierarchy; the very instruments we play have cultural connotations and differing status. Instruments used in rock'n'roll and popular music, for example, do not occupy the same territory as those of high culture: violins trump electric guitars, clarinets beat saxophones, classical music tops folk, pop and rock'n'roll. The formal music education system largely values and supports only those who read music, there is no parallel in Western classical music, for example, to the largely aural tradition of Indian classical music. And on it goes. Similarly we afford higher cultural value to certain modes of musical appreciation. Harmonic and melodic shapes and structures are prized above the rhythmic elements of music. Much pop music is based on grooves and feel, on repetitive patterns that allow us, in the words of James Brown, to 'get down'[2] and experience the earthier aspects of music, its physical and visceral dimensions. The music of Mozart on the other hand, while often listened to for its transcendent qualities, is praised from a more intellectual perspective for its technical sophistication and mastery of structure. These cultural values, both overt and implied, are absorbed into the psyche. Many of us grow up thinking that we are not musical, simply because we have not been exposed to formal music-making. We may sing to our children or to ourselves, but we would not call ourselves singers. This feeds the idea of the specialist and leads us to build structures around our art making that reflect this model. The actor-musician falls foul of this cultural framing and as a result is often perceived as being a lower-grade artist, neither a proper musician nor an actor, the result of financial necessity or expediency; little wonder that the form found its home within the alternative theatre movements.

If, as Blacking suggests, our understanding of musicianship is informed by a rarified or elitist view that results in a lack of recognition for musical skills that fall outside an imposed and narrow banding, then we need to re-evaluate and challenge the notion of specialism as it has been applied to music and music-making. The actor-musician in many ways is simply re-uniting two modes of communication: the semantic areas of language as codified meaning and its musical or prosodic elements. When we talk to one another we are managing a complex set of signals. It is often not what is being said, but how it is being spoken that reveals true meaning, body language plays its part in this, but so too does pitch, rhythm and timbre. The actor-musician is extending the natural interplay between musicality and language in their work. If we infer meaning from music, albeit a non-referential and poetic sense of meaning, then it would seem possible for an artist to use a musical instrument in tandem with their body and voice to express that meaning. Arguably this could even be seen as a more complete mode of expression, as Blacking suggests an act of mastery which understood on its own terms is equal to any expressed within the art music of the European tradition. The actor-musician by extension ceases to be the master of either skill and becomes instead expert in the combining of skills, the so-called jack and master.

For this expertise to be released and realized, however, it has to be recognized and honoured within the creative process and indeed within the training and development of the actor-musician. Maverick and radical directors such as Glen Walford and Bob Carlton have developed working methods that enable the actor-musician to flourish in the rehearsal room and on stage. Similarly John Doyle and Nikolai Foster's search for a means of reinvention has meant they are happy to embrace and explore new ways of working that use actor-musicianship as their starting point. In many cases, however, the pervading psychological-realist vocabularies of theatre making create a tension for the multi-skilled performer, placing the dilemma of actor-musicianship in the hands of the performer. As a result they have developed techniques and approaches to overcome this which have in turn become part of this act of mastery.

Acting and the actor-musician

At its worst being an actor-musician is like having a personality disorder. The performer is required to be two people at once. This may involve leaping on to stage from a dimly lit band area, hurriedly putting down your flute in order to deliver a few lines, before returning to play the next cue, or perhaps moving from a moment of stage action to an offstage or hidden band area to play music. This approach increases the tension between the disciplines. In the band area you identify as musician, the world is separate from the imagined world of the play, a place where only the music occurs, in isolation. You may still be in costume, but you are not part of the action of the play. The show, the director and it seems the audience has forgotten you. You are in David Roesner's words fulfilling the 'conventional expectations' we have for musicians in performance, that they are 'invisible, physically insignificant or transparent'.[3] You are of course free to behave in the way that musicians behave: you can disengage from the narrative and emotional flow of the play, you do not have to respond in character to the events around you, you can even use a music stand and do a crossword puzzle between cues. When on stage, however, you must engage once more with character, scenario and audience becoming in that sense visible once again. This dual existence is still common in productions that do not engage with actor-musicianship as a governing factor within their creation. The problem, if we choose to see it as such, is placed in the hands of the audience and performer.

For many actor-musicians this type of work may be unavoidable if they are to make a living, but it is certainly not rewarding. It accentuates the negative elements of their work, often leaving them feeling exploited and undervalued, unable to give full voice to their potential and left wondering if they are there simply to save the company the expense of a separate band. 'I feel trapped by my violin', 'I only got the job because I play the flute'[4] and comments like these are commonly heard from actor-musicians faced with this type of professional experience. For musical directors and sound designers it may be necessary for the music to happen within a designated band area, facilitating better listening and enabling more effective control of mics and fold back; however, if the music is being played by costumed actors who are also playing characters within the action of the piece, then the production is still asking its audience to include them in their reading of the performance. This perception may not always be considered or solved by the director, but you can be certain that it will be felt by the actor-musician in performance, giving rise to the question: 'Who am I when I am playing my trumpet?'[5] The question can of course be adapted to include other instruments.

In some shows, such as *Buddy*, *Pump Boys and Dinettes* or *From A Jack to a King* this is often, although not always, explained by the context. The actor-musician is playing a character, who within the legitimate action of the play happens to play the trumpet, at a rehearsal or gig re-enacted as part of the story for example. In many cases, however, this diegetic framing does not exist. The performer, still dressed as their character, is playing in support of a moment where their presence is not explained or suggested by the story. A binary diegetic or non-diegetic framing is not helpful in these instances, neither is the associated methodology of psychological realism. Who, therefore, are they when they are playing their trumpet? For many experienced actor-musicians this is a dilemma that they embrace without question, in the same way that audiences seem to. Loren O'Dair articulated her approach to those moments in the actor-musician musical *Once* in these terms: 'When you are at the side of the stage playing, you are the essence of your character'.[6] Actor-musician and co-founder of Dumbwise theatre company Eilidh deBonnaire sees this process as part and parcel of the actor-musician's job: 'Like all actors, the actor-musician is responsible for their own choices, which in their case includes the music.'[7] The music becomes part of the character's voice and the instrument, by extension part of their means of expression. Tom Wolstenholme, a recent graduate from Rose Bruford College's Actor Musicianship course, who also appeared in *Once*, explained it like this: 'I play an instrument in the way the piece wants me to play it.'[8] For most actor-musicians their instrument becomes part of the character; their process augments to include it in their thinking. With this, however, comes a set of technical challenges that once again highlights the very particular nature of the actor-musician's mastery.

Acting through the instrument

Most theatre musicians will use sheet music in performance, its presence, along with the associated music stand, creating a barrier between them and audience, preventing direct contact and interaction and limiting physical possibilities. As a result most actor-musician shows require the actor to perform the music from memory. This has become part of the appeal for audiences, but it has also created the need for a very distinctive skill. Musicians who work in rock, pop, folk or jazz may also work from memory, but often their music is freer in its form, unconnected to a narrative and with improvised passages and opportunities for soloing. Theatre scores by contrast are more structured affairs, requiring a level of consistency and a sense of story expressed through tempo, structure and dynamic, facilitated in the traditional theatre-pit-band-model by a conductor. For the actor-musician, however, there is no baton to follow. They rely instead on a collective understanding and sensitivity, governed by the dramaturgical ebb and flow of the piece itself. Actor-musicians as a result have to develop a very strong sense of ensemble, heightened listening skills and a sensitivity to the story as a whole. They have also to develop strategies for learning entire band parts. Being a competent reader of sheet music may well help during the early stages of rehearsals, but it is a skill that is rarely called on in performance. As a result actor-musician companies will often include readers and non- or limited readers within their ranks. Johnson Willis[9], for example, does not read music at all and yet has performed in many actor-musician shows, often mastering complex musical scores including *Carmen* and *Company*. He has a highly developed ability to play by ear, which sometimes slows things down in music rehearsals, but enables him to work freely when integrated into the scene, while readers in the cast are still weaning themselves off their scores.

With the music removed the actor-musician has also to find a new point of focus whilst playing. Actor-musicians in training and indeed in professional contexts can often struggle with this, defaulting to what we might call 'musician's eyes'. This refers to a sort of stare into the middle distance, which reveals more about the process of remembering and playing the notes, than anything to do with character or dramatic situation. To avoid this the actor-musician has to find a way of communicating through the music, of delivering action or attitude whilst playing. Actor-musicians have become adept at using a variety of approaches to facilitate this process. Many, encouraged by sensitive MDs and directors, might choose to explore the function of the music itself. Stephen Sondheim's music, for example, is peppered with moments where instruments and musical textures are used as a means of commenting on or supporting the action; brass lines or woodwind figures become wry comments or encouragement, rhythmic passages and instruments a means of driving a character or scene forward. The process of playing the music within a dramatic context, informed by the understanding of character and a relationship to the story, leads to all sorts of discoveries, as the actor's imagination is released into the extra-diegetic and poetic world that the music occupies. The actor or characters' eyes are then filled with the intentions and imagined worlds promoted by the coexistence of the music and the dramatic setting. Your character may not have a legitimate place within the scene, but 'their essence' can. In John Doyle's *Cabaret* at the Watermill, for example, the company of actor-musicians provided the musical accompaniment for Fraulien Schneider and Herr Schultz's heartwarming love song *Married*. Within the context of the story this is a private moment. In Doyle's version, however, the actor-musician band used their character's various perspectives to add new layers of meaning to the song. The cynical Kit Kat Girls mocked on violins and clarinet, whilst Cliff supported and drove the song with a gentle and fluid guitar, all over-shadowed by the haunting presence of the MC and his inevitable accordion. As with so many actor-musician bands the music had found its way into the inner life of the characters and the eyes, attitude and physicality of the performers. Susannah Van Den Berg's performance in Craig Revel Horwood's *Fiddler on the Roof* offers another example of this interplay. At one moment her character was engaged in a conver-sation with other members of the ensemble during a musical number. As she delivered a beautifully realized clarinet embellishment as part of Sarah Travis's spirited arrangements, her eyebrows lifted as if the musical figure were part of her character's vocal expression. The moment was apparently effortless and instinctive for the experienced actor-musician, but its playfulness delighted the audience, adding a layer of wit and informing the overwhelming sense that this was a very particular retelling of this well-known musical. For Van Den Berg, as for many practicing actor-musicians her focus as an actor has simply extended to include the instrument she plays and the music that comes from it.

For some it is the physicality of the instrument that offers a root into meaning and inner action. The physical act of playing double bass, for example, suggests an attitude all of its own. It is hard for directors and actor-musicians who play the instrument not to find themselves exploiting its characteristics within the gestus and physical language of the piece. Instruments can also become objects or props within the action, again offering an immediate attitude or relationship to inner life. Kelly O'Leary's cello became the baby her character Bertrande longed for in Craig Revel Horwood's version of *Martin Guerre*[10] and there have been several double bass horses in various productions, including John Doyle's *Moll Flanders.*

Once the eyes are activated there is another technical challenge that faces the actor-musician. Guitarists, pianists and accordion players are amongst the range of instrumentalists who have to learn to play without fixing their gaze on their fingers. It may not be immediately apparent, but it takes considerable skill and practice to deliver a complex guitar part whilst gazing into the eyes of another character or indeed at the audience; similarly to play, whilst singing, speaking and even dancing, which often delights audiences, but is the result of painstaking rehearsal and commitment from the actor-musician. Brass playing actor-musicians, in particular, have to be commended for their bravery; one false move or unplanned elbow and they are in danger of losing their teeth.

Actors first and foremost

As the term reflects actor-musicians are actors first: their ability to connect to and understand dramatic narrative, emotional stakes and dramaturgical shape is informed largely by this perspective. They may well be highly accomplished instrumentalists, indeed they often are, but they are not working in the same way that the professional theatre musician works. In the traditional musical theatre model, for instance, the band is brought together once the show has been rehearsed, working for only a few days before joining the cast for one glorious and often overwhelmingly beautiful moment known as the *sitzprobe*. The *sitzprobe*, or seated rehearsal as it translates from the German, is the moment when the orchestra come to the rehearsal space to facilitate the integration of the singing into their music, before retreating to the pit or band area, where they remain for the duration of the run, separated from company and audience, with only the conductor and musical director as a conduit between them and the stage action. The level and nature of skill required to facilitate this process is very different from that of the actor-musician, who has the entire rehearsal process to master the music. The sound and aesthetic of productions made in this way is also different. Here the physical presence of the musician plays no part in its reception, sound alone is the mode of artistic expression; for them there are no eyebrows to enhance or contextualize performance, instead they must deliver through the sensitivity and precision of their playing. As previously discussed they work under different contracts and different working conditions and inhabit a different culture within the theatre world. The band in many commercial musicals can often be seen in their blacks enjoying a cigarette or even a drink during the interval, while the actor, by contrast, remains in the dressing room, bound by conventions that forbid them to meet their audience outside the action of the play. They can be seen packing and unpacking their instruments in the pit, exchanging looks and comments on occasion and generally engaging in activity that lies outside of the imagined world of the production. They are in that sense one step closer to the audience and one step removed from the action and the cast; their skill set is different, the outcomes they enable unlike those of the actor-musician. This is not to say that musicians cannot become actors. There are examples of companies such as The Gogmagogs and the work of Matthew Sharpe,[11] which explore how music-making by classically trained musicians can be used as the starting point for performance. David Roesner and Matthias Rebstock's book *Composed Theatre*[12] explores this notion, reflected here in this extract from an article written for *Studies in Musical Theatre*:

> The subject of my article therefore is not only the various uses of (incidental) music in theatre, but a wider range of developments,

in which principles of music are applied to the expressive means of the theatre or at times – vice versa – the 'theatricalization' of making music.[13]

This process of theatricalizing the making of music is certainly part of actor-musicianship; for actor-musicians, however, it is the primary sensitivity of the actor that is brought to bear on the music-making rather than that of the musician. For those musicians who venture into acting the journey can be quite different. Paddy Cunneen recalls seeing a musician colleague joining the stage action in a production at London's National Theatre.[14] He was struck by how awkward his presence appeared in contrast to the physical life of the actors surrounding him. There was something about the very act of being present within the dramatic frame that the musician was unable to match, that sense of heightened reality that exists even in productions that we might describe as naturalistic in style.

How audiences read actor-musicianship

Bert Olen States[15] suggests that when we go to the theatre we buy into a contract with the performer, behaving and responding in ways that are part and parcel of a form of cultural conditioning that governs our responses. For States there are a series of modes that define this relationship between performer and audience. The 'self-expressive mode' sees the performer as virtuoso, in possession of skills that we are asked to sit back and marvel at and enjoy. It is into this mode that the classical music performance can stray. The 'collaborative mode' refers to the act of collusion between actor and audience. This mode is present in most narrative theatre and indeed in all performance models that require the audience to engage with an imagined world. It is activated immediately in the act of soliloquy or in the actor's use of 'you' as means of addressing the audience. Finally 'the representational mode' is at play when we read the signs offered to us by a production. A box on the stage may become a chair or table, a train or car. In fact everything we see on the stage, actors included, are in some way representational; a chair when on stage is representing a chair within the imagined world of the play, the actor representing a character. These modes are of course not mutually exclusive and indeed in actor-musicianship we see them all at play. The audience 'collaborate' in an acceptance that the actors are both existing within the given circumstances of the imagined world of the play, while playing instruments that are servicing the delivery of a performance, they in that sense participate in the act of actor-musicianship. They may well be impressed by the level of skills being demonstrated by the performers, tapping into the 'self-expressive mode' as they applaud the sheer circus-like appeal of witnessing a company act, sing, play and perhaps dance their way through a musical number. Finally the 'representation mode' is at play as the audience read and interpret the various signals sent by the presence of the instruments: the double bass is welcomed as the highwayman's horse, Bertrande's cello read as her unborn baby. In this sense audiences accept and delight in actor-musicianship and actor-musicians, in turn, combine the vocabularies of musical performance and acting in an instinctive and effortless exchange. They are both in that sense complicit, as States suggests:

> Behind the representational mode of performance and our perception of it, is the shared sense that we come to the theatre primarily to see a play and not a performance.[16]

In this sense, the play is where the shared endeavour lies – the narrative framing that enables actor-musicianship to ignite within the collective imagination of the audience and performer.

Musicality and the actor-musician

'Musicality in theatre has the potential ... to act as a catalyst between theatre and music'[17] David Roesner suggests. We could say that it is the underlying sensitivity that unites the two skills of acting and music-making. Its presence in music may be self evident, but acting methodologies and performance also draw on ideas of musicality. In comedy, for example, a sense of rhythm and an understanding of musical shape is crucial in the delivery of non-musical material. Similarly many actors and directors understand how musical ideas such as flow and tempo can inform dramatic action. A scene or exchange can be transformed simply by instructing actors to close the gaps and work faster or indeed create more space and work at a slower tempo. It is here in the inner world of musicality that we find the hidden territory[18] where the skills of the actor and the musician meet. No surprise then that many acting methodologies contain references to musicality: from Stanislavski's notion of rhythm and tempo to Meyerhold's Eurhythmics, from Michael Chekov's ideas about atmosphere to Staniewski's use of the term as a central tenet within his work.

If the actor-musician can be defined as an *actor* who plays an instrument, then what of the musician part of the equation? We have explored several examples of how the two disciplines can interrelate, but it is also necessary for the musical elements of their mastery to be enabled. Music in most actor-musician contexts has to be rehearsed, at least in part, in separate music calls. Here the very particular qualities of the music such as discovering shape, achieving balance and dynamic shifts are explored using orthodox musical approaches. Just as there are points in most actor-musician processes where one might find the cast engaged in what we could primarily identify as acting tasks, such as scene reading and work on the meaning of text, so there are moments when the needs of the musician must lead. Music rehearsals are often seated and the one occasion where the cast might work from musical scores or band parts. They are also usually led by the MD who may conduct in order to help the group find, and explore, shape and dynamics, which they must later repeat in performance without such guidance. The culture of these rehearsals is often very different from work that focuses on integration. Much like the 'table-work' that precedes 'floor work' in a text-based actor's process, it is a chance to unpick and understand the music, an intellectually focused activity in large degree. These rehearsals, however, will often be informed by acting processes; discoveries made in the rehearsal of scenes may begin to shape the music, with adjustments frequently being made by both MDs and performers based on their understanding of the physical and emotional life of the character or scene. Equally discoveries made in the music rehearsals might colour the acting and staging, new connections between the score and the world of the play are frequently being discovered as the actor's imagination remains active, quietly watching and listening as the 'musician' rehearses. The shapes found in the music rehearsal form and echo dramaturgical shape found in the scenes. This part of the process may be focused solely on the making of music, or sometimes prosaic and pragmatic activities such as note-bashing to facilitate learning, but the 'actor' side of the equation is always present. Used to its full advantage it is also a useful rehearsal for the extended creative team, who, unlike in traditional musical theatre models, are offered a chance to hear the musical world of the piece being constructed, enabling their work to be informed and shaped by the process and vice-versa. Choreographer Steven Hoggett[19] and lighting designer Richard G Jones[20] both use music rehearsals as a stimulus for their work, another example of how the processes that surround actor-musicianship offer a very particular means of integration.

A different type of actor

The duality of their skill-set shapes the actor-musician, as do the processes they have to balance within the creation of work. Managing the learning of lines and music and the need to switch between modes of rehearsal engenders discipline and flexibility. There is a distinct sense of ensemble found in actor-musician companies that is not always replicated in casts of actors. John Doyle talked of an increased sense of ownership that he finds in actor-musician companies,[21] similarly Paddy Cunneen talked of the 'subjugation of the ego'[22] and a propensity for self-reflection that he locates in the musical make-up of the actor-musician:

> For me there is huge difference between acting and music in one key area, which is that music is an objective discipline … you can sit down at the piano and invent a new way of playing it and that's great, but ultimately there's an objective thing there that enables you to tell, as you are working, whether it is any good or not. You can tell whether that melody sings properly; whether your technique is good enough. And the objectivity of that makes you work harder, gives you feedback all the time about yourself and encourages you to criticize yourself, cause you know that the more you criticize yourself, the better you get. And as much as your teachers rap your knuckles, eventually when they stop doing that, you find that you are rapping your own knuckles and now you are making progress.

Actor-musicianship is an ensemble theatre form. The productions largely require the company to be on stage or at least witnessing the stage action throughout, a fact reflected in the rehearsal process. The rehearsal schedule that one finds in much mainstream theatre practice may list only the actors required to play the characters in the scene being rehearsed. In actor-musician processes this is rarely the case, as the full company has to be present most of the time, as the scene expands to include those actors required to play the music and, therefore, be included in the stage action. As a result actor-musicians may end up working longer hours than other actors, but they in turn develop a stronger sense of company and ownership.

Roles within actor-musician cast groups can also become less clearly defined. The early Rhythm Method[23] shows, for example, would include what became known as the 'Parish Pump' as part of the daily pre-show warm-up. This was a chance for the whole cast, and often crew, to discuss the previous night's show, suggesting areas that needed to be worked on and offering notes on music and songs. This is a very different model from that found in other mainstream theatre practices, where performance notes are given only by those with designated roles, such as director, MD or their assistants. The practice continued in many actor-musician contexts, including John Doyle's early work at the Watermill. This sense of collective responsibility is an important characteristic of actor-musician companies and is reflective more of musical contexts than acting. As Paddy Cunneen suggests there is something about the objectivity of music that enables band members to offer notes to one another that help to release and develop musical processes. In an acting context, however, similar strategies can often present problems; giving notes on acting choices, is somehow a much more politically and emotionally dangerous act. This tension can be increased for actor-musicians who find themselves being asked to operate both as a member of the company and as an in-house MD or musical supervisor. This is particularly common amongst mixed cast groups of actor and actor-musicians. The problem is twofold. First the split focus in performance can increase the sense of tension between the skill sets; instead of giving themselves up to the moment and serving the collective endeavour, the performer is required to monitor and analyse the piece and the work of others. Secondly the giving of notes from within company can often promote tensions; it is an unspoken rule in many traditional theatre-making processes that actors do not

give notes to other actors. Once again the processes that govern
actor-musicianship are distinctive and not always transferable.

Working as an actor-musician

Actor-musicians can find themselves in a wide range of performance
and professional contexts. Much of the work we have focused on
thus far could be classed as musical theatre or perhaps music-theatre
that utilizes a company predominantly made up of actor-musicians,
but work can also be found within casts predominantly consisting
of actors and within productions that, although they may contain
musical elements, would not be defined as musicals; as we will
discuss later there is also an extensive use of actor-musicians within
theatre for children and young people. These various contexts require
differing approaches from these most flexible of performers.

While the ambition of most actor-musicians is to undertake jobs
that primarily honour their identity as actors, this is not always the
case. In order to stay in work actor-musicians can find themselves
in shows that call mainly on their musical prowess. This sort of work
can often feel exploitative and in some cases is clearly more suited
to professional musicians. Examples might include the offstage band
given bit-parts or the presence of a costumed instrumentalist who is
really only incidental to the dramatic action. In many cases it is the
instruments themselves that dictate or limit the performer's dramatic
function. Drum-kit playing actor-musicians, for example, are often
unable to escape from the rather overwhelming physical reality of
their instrument. Equally pianists can find themselves inhibited by
the static nature of their discipline. Many choose to find doubles that
complement their primary instrument and enhance the possibility
of integration: pianists often find their way onto accordion and kit
drummers explore various hand-held options. Similarly those who
play instruments that have limited or very specific use may choose

to augment their skills by learning instruments that share some of the same characteristics or techniques. Classically trained clarinetists and flautists often move onto saxophone, which has similar fingering and, in the case of the clarinet, shares the single-reed. Guitarists take up other fretted instruments such as banjo and ukulele and electric bass players often migrate to double bass in order to make themselves more employable. Certainly in the UK it seems there is work for all sorts of instrumentalists and for all physical types and ages. Sarah Travis's arrangements for *Fiddler on the Roof* even saw the need for a bassoon, a newcomer to the actor-musician scene. Similarly the propensity of guitarists means that only the best and more versatile tend to work consistently. But actor-musicianship is a balancing act. For every MD looking for a particular instrumental line-up there is a director wanting to find the best acting talent they can. As we will explore in later chapters the process of casting and balancing skills within an actor-musician show is a complex and multi-faceted process and so with the range and extent of work currently available in the UK at least, it is little wonder that actor-musicians of all types are in high demand.

Singing and the actor-musician

One of the skills often, although not always, required in actor-musician performance is that of singing. In many ways singing is the perfect act of actor-musicianship, offering the opportunity to express musically without the abstraction of an instrument. Actor-musician work is perhaps a little more forgiving and wide-ranging in the type of singers and singing it requires. Given the range of possible contexts there is room for many different styles and type of voice. Musical theatre training programmes in the UK and America teach singing predominantly within the Estill[24] method, which encourages a range of vocal qualities that have become part and parcel of the somewhat ubiquitous musical theatre sound and aesthetic. As actor-musicianship begins to compete in the commercial arena with mainstream musicals, it is becoming increasingly necessary for actor-musician performers to produce this type of vocal sound. John Doyle has identified an increasing stable of actor-musicians in the US who are accomplished singers, actors and instrumentalists, often adding dance to their list of credentials, thus giving credence to the idea of the 'quadruple threat'. This term, which grew out of the American musical theatre idea of the 'triple threat' referring to the performer who could sing, dance and act, is not particularly helpful when applied to actor-musicianship. It speaks to the agenda of the specialist, suggesting a performer who can compete on four levels simultaneously: they dance as well as any dancer, they sing and play as well as a singer or musician and of course act their socks off to boot. This uber-artist may seem a desirable commodity, but the acquisition of skills should be neither the goal nor the criterion that we use to measure artistic merit. Actor-musicianship is perhaps better viewed as a singular discipline with its own particular outcome and associated aesthetic.

Actor-musicians in America

In the USA the notion of the specialist actor-musician is perhaps less well defined. For American actors musicianship has simply become another skill to acquire or brush up. Alex Gemignani, who played the Beadle in John Doyle's *Sweeney Todd*, is perhaps typical of the new breed of actor-musician currently working in the States. Although starting life as a musician Gemignani went on to become an acting major at college, finally launching himself as a musical theatre actor-singer after graduation. He had undertaken a number of roles when John Doyle's *Sweeney Todd* first began casting in the US. He recalls the audition process that saw actors from across New York dusting off long-forgotten instruments in preparation. Despite previous Broadway productions of *Planet* and *Buddy* plus the homegrown *Pump Boys and Dinettes* actor-musicianship was still a relatively new concept to Gemignani's generation of actor. There had been call from time to time for guitar or harmonica playing in shows, but not for orchestral instruments. Patti LuPone also recalls having to play instruments in shows during her career, but never to the extent that Doyle and Travis encouraged. There is perhaps less recognition of the idea of the actor-musician in American theatre culture, but as a result of John Doyle's ground-breaking approach to integrating instruments and the follow-on successes of John Tiffany's long-running actor-musician musical *Once* American musical theatre performers began to recognize the need to maintain and develop musical skills alongside their talents as actors, singers and dancers, and there are now examples of actor-musician based theatre across the country.

The specific cultural context within which American actors operate dictates that there is both a high level of skill and competition to achieve the equally high financial rewards that a job within the American commercial theatre sector can afford. Both Kate Edgar and Bob Carlton recalled the scale of the task when auditioning for the off-Broadway debut of *Return to the Forbidden Planet*. The long list of American auditionees included many who went to extraordinary lengths to prepare for what was to them a new theatre form, learning instruments to very high standards and some even flying to London to see the show. Actor-musicianship, as a very British take on the musical form, has a different agenda. John Doyle, while applauding the skills at his disposal, is keen to encourage his American actor-musicians to take risks, asking them to stop 'trying to be perfect' as only then, he suggests, will they find something different and fresh.[25] Actor-musicianship it seems, even in its most recent incarnation, still asks its performers to be innovators.

A new approach to performance

When Tom Spencer's company Fine Chisel were approached by the MTN Awards to be recipients of Best New Musical for their show *Dumbstruck* they refused, worried that it would associate them with the mainstream musical theatre movement. They played to a young and progressive audience who were attracted by the hybridity of this theatre-company-come-band, who perform in pubs and music festivals as well as theatre venues. In response MTN created a new category of award in innovation, which Tom was happy to accept. For Tom Spencer, as for Glen Walford and Joan Littlewood before him, actor-musicianship is a way of attracting new audiences and of exploring fresh ways of making theatre. The polish of the commercial musical is certainly something that many actor-musicians and actor-musician shows can match, but the actor-musician brings with them something rougher and more visceral that, as John Blacking suggests, taps into the very core of what it means to share music and music-making.

Actor-musicianship is certainly a broad church. As with most things the better and more versatile you are in terms of the range and type of skills you possess then potentially the more employable you will be. But with actor-musicianship now being found in so many places and forms it seems that there is room for almost any permutation of instrument, voice and physical type. Rather than a jack-of-all-trades, the actor-musician is master of the combining of skills; of acting through their music-making, of using music to enhance and support acting. Those performers like Karen Mann, who have made their careers almost entirely within the actor-musician world, have developed a set of skills that are particular. The work of actor-musicians may be multi-faceted, but it can still be characterized as a craft in its own right. This singular craft has rarely been recognized and defined, even by those who work within the sector. Actor-musicians have generally been too busy finding work and often complaining about why they are only being cast because they play an instrument, to realize that the very fact that they play that instrument as an integrated part of their creative·expression is the very thing that makes them unique and so eminently employable. It is in the act of playing and acting that they are actually practising and developing a mastery, which, for the time being at least, seems to chime with the zeitgeist of contemporary theatre culture. Once again from Birmingham to Broadway mainstream theatres seems to be embracing hybridity. The National Theatre's extraordinary success with a puppet show, *War Horse*, is just one indication of how times have changed. How we define and characterize the mode and aesthetic of our theatre may always be in flux but, from the anti-dramatic to the highly theatrical, there seems never to have been a better time for Ewan MacColl's vision of the multi-faceted performer. As he reminds us, however, 'it is one thing to have a desire, but another thing to carry that desire into practice'.[26] If we are to truly embrace and develop actor-musicianship we need to recognize the very particular processes and training mechanisms needed to nurture and develop it. As Philip Zarilli suggests 'new directorial approaches or ways of structuring the tasks of the actor require new approaches to acting'.[27]

Notes

1 Blacking, J., *How Musical is Man?* (Seattle: University of Washington Press, 1973), 4.

2 Soul singer and rhythm and blues legend James Brown used the phrase 'get down' in a number of songs including his 1971 recording of *Soul Power*: 'Don't fall on the ground, we got to get down, Down, down, down, down ...'. The phrase refers to the descent into the physical and indeed meta-physical dimensions and rhythmic power of his music. Funk and soul music was a dance music that grew out of the African American experience. The phrase suggests and echoes with the ritual roots of much African music, which in turn connects to the deeper resonances that music has for humans, its connection to the physical and spiritual.

3 Roesner, D. (2010), 'Musicking as *mise-en-scene*, Studies in Musical
   Theatre 4:1', *Studies in Musical Theatre* 4 (1) (August 2010): 93, doi:
   10.1386/smt.4.1.89_1. Further discussion of this convention can also be
   found in Small, C., *Musiking: The Meanings of Performing and Listening*
   (Hanover: University Press of New England, 1998), and in Barnett, D.,
   The Performance of Music: A Study in Terms of Pianoforte (London:
   Barrie and Jenkins, 1972).

4 These and many similar comments have been made both during
   productions and at forum events run by the author. It is not appropriate
   to credit them to individuals. However, recordings of some of
   these events are available from the Rose Bruford College research
   department.

5 This question and ones similar have been heard in rehearsal rooms at
   Rose Bruford College and in professional contexts experienced by the
   author throughout his career.

6 Loren O'Dair played Reza in the second cast of *Once* in the West End.
   She did not experience the original rehearsal process and so many of
   the solutions she came up with were informed by her own judgements
   about how best to manage the potential dilemma posed by playing
   an instrument in moments when her character's presence may not
   have been explained by the narrative. Interestingly O'Dair trained at Le
   Coq and so was not subject to the same emphasis on psychological
   realism as one finds in text based training models. Instead her training
   pedagogy was informed by devising and physical theatre models.
   This quote is taken from Jack and Master: Actor-musicianship in
   Performance and Process, a research forum held at The Bargehouse, 6
   June 2014.

7 Eilidh deBonnaire trained on Rose Bruford College's Actor Musicianship
   programme. She is performer, MD and composer for Dumbwise theatre
   company and has worked as an actor-musician in a number of contexts,
   including for The Almeida's outreach team. This quote was taken from
   Jack and Master: Actor-musicianship in Performance and Process, a
   research forum led by Jeremy Harrison at The Bargehouse, 6 June 2014.

8 Tom Wolstenholme speaking at Jack and Master: Actor-musicianship in
   Performance and Process, The Bargehouse, 6 June 2014.

9 Jonson Willis is a UK-based actor-musician who has worked extensively
   within the form at theatres including Theatr Clwyd, The Watermill,
   Ipswich's New Wolsey and in the West End. He has worked with many

of the leading figures of the UK actor-musician scene including John Doyle, Peter Rowe and Tim Baker and for MDs Sarah Travis, Catherine Jayes and Greg Palmer.

10 In July 2007 Craig Revel Horwood directed an actor-musician reworking of Claude-Michel Schonberg and Alain Boublil's musical *Martin Guerre,* with musical arrangements by Sarah Travis at The Watermill Theatre. The actor-musician cast included Kelly O'Leary as Bertrande do Rois, Ben Goddard as Martin Guerre and veteran actor-musician Karen Mann as Madame de Rois.

11 The work of Lucy Bailey and Nell Catchpole's Gogmagogs, a company of classically trained musicians, has been cited in Chapter 1, along with classical cellist and singer Matthew Sharpe, whose output has included work with composer Pete M. Wyer under their collective name Sharpwire.

12 Rebstock, M. and Roesner, D. eds., *Composed Theatre: Aesthetics, Practices, Processes* (Bristol: Intellect Books, 2012).

13 Roesner, D. (2010), 'Musicality as a Paradigm for the Theatre: A Kind of Manifesto', *Studies in Musical Theatre 4:3,* 294, doi: 10.1386/smt.4.3.293_1.

14 Paddy Cunneen in conversation with Jeremy Harrison for the purposes of this publication on 12 September 2014.

15 O. States, B. (2002), *The Actor's Presence: Three Phenomenal Modes,* in P. Zarrilli, ed., *Acting (Re)Considered* (Abingdon: Routledge, 2002), Part. 1, Ch. 2.

16 Ibid., 33.

17 See note 12.

18 In this context the phrase refers to the work of Gardzienice as explored in Alison Hodge's book of the same name: Hodge, A. ed., *Hidden Territories: The Theatre of Gardzienice* (Abingdon: Routledge, 2003).

19 Steven Hoggett is an internationally renowned choreographer and founder of physical theatre company Frantic Assembly. In this context his work on the actor-musician musical *Once* is being cited, as discussed in conversation with Jeremy Harrison during an interview conducted for this publication on 6 August 2014. The specific examples referred to are discussed in detail in later chapters.

20 Richard G. Jones has been a long-time collaborator with John Doyle, lighting the majority of his actor-musician productions throughout the

1980s, 1990s and early 2000s. He lit both the Broadway and West End productions of *Sweeney Todd.* He has since collaborated with other actor-musician directors including Craig Revel Horwood. The example cited here was discussed in conversation with Jeremy Harrison in an interview conducted for this publication on 10 April 2014, as part of a symposium event held at Rose Bruford College.

21 John Doyle in conversation with Jeremy Harrison in an interview conducted for this publication on 26 March 2014.

22 Paddy Cunneen in conversation with Jeremy Harrison in an interview conducted for this publication on 12 September 2014.

23 Rhythm Method, as discussed in Chapter 1, was set up by Bob Carlton and members of his original Bubble company, including Matt Devitt, Kate Edgar, John Ashby, Annie Miles and Bobby Aitken. Christian Roberts, an actor producer, and actress Alison Harding also joined as newcomers for their first production at the 1983 Edinburgh Festival. The company stayed together throughout the early 1990s and co-produced the West End productions of *Return to the Forbidden Planet* and *From A Jack to a King,*

24 Jo Estill was a singing coach who developed her distinctive teaching method during the 1980s following an extended period of research. The technique, which focuses on the development of a series of vocal qualities, which include 'twang' and 'belt', has become synonymous with the musical theatre vocal sound. Her techniques form the basis of most singing teaching found in conservatoires within the UK and America. Her work has been disseminated through a series of books by teachers who follow her principles including UK-based Gillyanne Kayes, whose book co-incidentally carries a picture of Jo Baird playing Sally Bowles in John Doyle's actor-musician production of *Cabaret* on its front cover: Kayes, G., *Singing and the Actor* (Abingdon: Routledge, 1999).

25 John Doyle in conversation with Jeremy Harrison in an interview undertaken for this publication; see note 7.

26 Ewan MacColl recorded talking about Theatre Union, broadcast as part of *Archive on 4: Joan Littlewood and the People's Theatre*, presented by Sir Richard Eyre, broadcast on BBC Radio 4, 8 p.m. 27 September 2014.

27 Zarrilli, P. ed., *Acting (Re)Considered* (London: Routledge, 2002), 19.

3

TRAINING THE
ACTOR-MUSICIAN:
AN INTRODUCTION

This chapter functions as a response to the call from Phillip Zarrilli that closed our last section, in that it outlines a 'new approach' to actor training that is focused at developing actor-musicianship as a singular and distinctive skill. It is important to acknowledge that there are occasions when musical and acting skills can and indeed should be developed in isolation, actor-musicians require approaches to the breaking down and understanding of text, for example, and to physical and vocal flexibility and release as applied to the training of all actors. They also need space to develop discrete musical skills, such as ensemble music-making and the flexibility and technical command required to approach a variety of different musical styles. Nonetheless actor-musicianship requires a means of embracing the act of music-making as an integrated and embodied element of acting and this is something that can and should be trained and developed. With the demand for actor-musicians increasing, drama schools and acting courses are starting to create training pathways that encourage this sort of interdisciplinary. With the notion of specialism still largely governing much conservatoire practice, however, it is not clear how such a process should be encouraged, with many separating the elements in training, only bringing them together in project work or performance. This can lead to an accentuating of the tension between the disciplines, leaving it solely in the hands of the actor-musician to generate the act of integration, with many of the staff and practitioners leading this work being unclear how to assess and support the process. Rose Bruford College was the first drama school to embrace actor-musicianship, creating a training programme in the 1990s which was based on an augmentation of the pedagogies relating to actor training, rather than a marriage to those found in music conservatoire practice, although inevitably there are areas where the two may overlap. Music classes or instrumental lessons play their part, but a curriculum aimed at the actor-musician as singular artist must be balanced in such a way that it does not compromise the primary development of the actor, nor lead to the intensifying of tension between the two skills. Experience of training actor-musicians at Rose Bruford College has shown that the musical elements of their training, when approached with this in mind, can enhance acting skills, and that musical skills can in turn be strengthened by the application of perspectives informed by acting, a fact born out in many professional contexts. Musical director and composer Paddy Cunneen's extensive work with actor-musicians, for instance, has led him to conclude that the knowledge they have as actors improves their ability to operate as musicians, allowing them to shape music in response to stage action and with a sensitivity to emotional and narrative undercurrents. In short, done in the right way, the two disciplines are interrelated and can be developed in tandem.

What follows then is a collection of exercises and working methods that focus on what we might define as the singular skill of actor-musicianship: the jack as master, to borrow from the vocabulary of the previous chapter. There is existing precedence for many of the ideas we will encounter and where possible I have provided a context and provenance. It is, however, largely an account of approaches developed in my own practice and as a result many of the ideas have been borrowed, reinvented or bastardized and in some cases it is hard to remember where and how they first came about. They are all, however, deeply rooted in a practical experience of training and working with professional actor-musicians over 27 years, informed by a theoretical underpinning that I would like to begin by outlining.

Musicality as a training methodology

It is in the notion of musicality that we find the meeting place of the actor and the musician. This largely internal landscape is central to the human experience, but hard to define within a performance or theatre-making context or indeed as part of a training methodology. In his article 'Musicality as a Paradigm for the Theatre: A Kind of Manifesto' David Roesner offers a helpful starting point:

> While the term 'musical' can refer both to the ability of some*one* as well as the characteristic of some*thing*, the noun 'musicality' is almost exclusively used to describe a human talent … I would like to suspend restricting the term to human talent, enabling me to apply the notion to things, situations and processes, so that it becomes meaningful to speak of a musicality of the theatre, of a particular staging or lighting design, of a rehearsal or of the musicality of an act of representation. The second dissolution of a boundary is indebted to the music pedagogue Heinrich Jacoby … He put forward a notion of musicality as being a general expressive capacity of all human beings, comparable to their mother tongue. Consequently, the notion of a musicality in theatre, as an art form and as the theatrical event itself, would refer to the intrinsic affinity of the stage to music, with which it was, so to speak, issued at birth. Striving towards a musicality in theatre is thus perhaps less a case of learning and training, but an act of excavating and 'liberating'.[1]

Musicality for the actor-musician becomes a process and outcome, a latent inner landscape and sensitivity requiring liberation and exploration. It is an idea commonly found as an underpinning element of actor training practices, such as in Stanislavski's ideas of tempo and rhythm, and an approach exploited by a number of directors who use musical vocabulary to help shape and guide performance work. How often, for example, do we hear directors talking about timing or the rhythmic or dynamic shape of a scene, offering musical analogy as a means of encouraging dramaturgical or dramatic shape and form? It is perhaps most prominent, however, in the work of Polish theatre company Gardzienice and the associated working methods of its director and founder Wlodzimierz Staniewski. For him musicality is a central tenet that he defines as follows:

> Everything which sounds beyond the 'edges' of the codified system is musicality... This is because music represents a certain level of abstraction, whereas musicality can be immediately identified as something that sits inside of me, or something that I hear in real life. Musicality is me.[2]

Both Roesner and Staniewski suggest an almost archeological endeavor and indeed when considering the inner musicality of the actor, we have to acknowledge that musicality is central to the human experience.

There have been many accounts of the role of music in mankind's development, but perhaps one of the most comprehensive and compelling can be found in archaeologist Steven Mithen's book *The Singing Neanderthals*. In it he offers a detailed account of how our evolutionary history has created a deep link between music and the very structures of the brain. He posits a theory of a proto-language that he calls 'Hmmmmm' which formed the basis of communication in early man, before we developed a codified language of semantics. The legacy of this, Mithen suggests, is that our brains still process music as having meaning, attached to its now latent function as a primary vehicle of communication:

> The modules [of the brain] related to pitch organization would once have been central to 'Hmmmmm', but are now recruited only for music ... while other 'Hmmmmm' modules might now be recruited largely for the language system alone – perhaps, for example, those relating to grammar. This evolution history explains how brain injuries can affect either music alone, language alone or both systems if some shared modules are damaged.[3]

'Hmmmmm', he points out, is still applied in some modes of human communication, such as Infant Directed Speech (IDS), where we prioritize the prosodic, musical elements of language over the semantic. An extended use of pitch and rhythmic emphasis becomes our instinctive response when talking to preverbal children and indeed animals, often embarrassingly straying into our engagement with those who speak other languages, telling us that if we simply repeat words with more physical animation, vocal colour and volume then we will be understood. 'Hmmmmm', like musicality, is the place where music and language meet, and by extension it reflects our ability to blend semantic and referential systems of meaning, with broader sensorial, poetic and non-referential meanings that we infer from music. It is evidence of how music is central to the way we receive and project meaning and in this way it connects to John Blacking's arguments about musical specialism presented earlier. It is a reminder that the processes of music-making and speaking are interrelated; we are in this sense all engaged in acts of music-making when we communicate with one another. IDS is just one example of how musical meaning is explored explicitly in our engagements, the lullaby, which is an extension of this idea, is perhaps another worth briefly exploring.

Lullabies exist in all human cultures, they can be traced back to as early as 2000 BC[4] and can still be heard in most households where a young, and crucially pre-verbal, child or baby lives. In the lullaby we see the complete power of musicality being harnessed: the baby is sung to in gentle tones, using words that they do not understand, but that provide a narrative and linguistic context for the adult singer; melody and timbre are shaped by the action of inducing sleep, the rhythmic structures too, the singer may offer a rocking motion that extends and deepens the experience into a full body sensation. Why do we do this? Well the answer is simple, because it works. We are harnessing the power that music has to change those who listen to it. In the case of the lullaby we are literally changing someone from a person who is awake, and maybe crying, into someone who is asleep and quiet. This act of transformation is instinctive and yet it provides evidence of the complex way in which musical actions inform the way we communicate. Any approach to facilitating interaction between the two skills of music and acting, therefore, needs to be located in this latent area of our consciousness. The process may well be one of liberation, but like so many approaches to the training of actors it is fundamentally about enabling and releasing instinctive behaviours and sensitivities. Actor-musicianship has at its core the shared endeavour of music-making and speaking as interrelated modes of communication and expression. Add to this the strong connectivity between music and movement and it is clear that the notion of musicality can encompass the key areas targeted in conservatoire actor training models: voice, movement and approaches to text and inner life, that we might define as acting skills. For actor-musicians the addition of music to this triumvirate of core skills is necessary, but what is important is that musical development is managed in such a way that it is fostered by and connected to the other areas of the actor's work. Musicality is present in all areas of acting and as such it is a relatively simple step to expose and heighten its existence in such a way that it can lead, or at least co-exist with, text, voice and body as a primary process for the training and developing of work using actor-musicians.

Exercises and training methods for actor-musicians

The exercises and working methods outlined in the next section will be divided into two parts: one which looks at the development of musicality, followed by a section on how musicality can be applied in performance and as part of the actor's approach to text, character and inner life.

They have been grouped into thematic areas and in many cases into primary exercises and follow-on activity. The musicality work is largely experiential training and designed to build a group's ability and levels of sensitivity across several sessions. Preliminary exercises can be repeated and developed using the follow-on activities. There is a suggestion of development in the order that they have been set out, but they can be adapted and re-ordered depending on the context.

Most of the musicality exercises rely on a fluid teaching style, with one exercise designed to flow into the next. Any instructions from the facilitator are to be given whilst the group is engaged in an activity, so encouraging a level of focus that enables this way of working may be necessary.

The application exercises are more independent of one another and so can form the basis for workshop or one-off lessons or rehearsal techniques. As part of a curriculum for training actor-musicians they are best used in combination, with sensitizing musicality work being used to open up and engage a group, followed by some application work that offers a context for learning.

In the end they are offered for you to use in any way that seems appropriate for your setting and as a provocation for those wishing to explore how musical ideas can be used as a starting point in acting processes.

Fostering musicality

These exercises are designed to help reconnect and awaken sensitivities to music or musicality that inform the way we communicate and receive meaning. They are offered within the context of this book as a training methodology for actor-musicians, but they can be applied to the training of any actor. Later exercises will include the use of musical instruments, but many of the core exercises rely solely on the ability to work with rhythm and sung sound. Although designed for use within an actor-training context, many of the exercises are also suitable for work with young people, adult theatre groups and professional actors. I have endeavoured to offer guidelines for their use in terms of possible target groups and function, but these should only be seen as suggestions.

Listening as physical action – an introduction to musicality

Overview

This first exercise is aimed at training-actors or adults and young people of 15 years of age and over. It is not necessarily an exercise that one would do as an opening activity as it is quite sedentary, but I offer it as our first exercise because it is not too challenging, as it is close to the ways in which we engage with music in our day-to-day lives. It speaks to what John Blacking describes as the 'essential processes' of music that can be 'found in the constitution of the human body'[5] and is an illustration of what Anthony Storr describes as the 'closer relationship between *hearing* and emotional arousal'.[6]

Requirements

1 A group of two or more people.

2 Each individual will need to bring a music playing device and headphones, and a recording of a piece of music that means something to them. It may be a piece that relates to a moment in their own lives or that promotes a particular feeling or emotional quality – it may be worth asking that no one brings anything that is very long, such as a symphony.

The exercise:

- Begin with a discussion about how and why we listen to music:

   a) How many tracks or pieces of music do the members of the group have on their phones or iPods?

   b) How do they choose which songs to listen to and when?

   c) Do they listen to music depending on mood or for activities such as sport or preparing for a night out and if so what dictates the choice of music for each occasion?

- The discussion should allow the group to begin to acknowledge and explore the ways they use music in their everyday lives, to recognize what we could describe as its 'extra-musical' properties. A reminder of just how complex our relationship to listening is.

- A member of the group is selected to be watched as they listen to their choice of music (you could choose to divide the group into pairs who alternate in this activity if that works better for you and them).

- The group observe in silence.

- Allow some distance between those observing and the listener.

- Encourage the listener to open their eyes for at least some of the exercise.

- The group must observe everything that they notice in the listener, even the smallest changes.

- This is followed by a discussion of what was observed.

- The exercise can then be repeated for as long as the group can focus or enjoy it.

- It may also be interesting for the group to hear the music once the observation is completed.

Outcomes

The outcomes of this exercise are largely dependent on the listener. Responses can vary from very subtle changes in the pattern of breathing and small shifts in facial expression, to more pronounced physical changes, such as a shifting in the spine or strong intakes of breath. What is certain is that nobody will listen to an entire piece of music that has meaning to them without it finding its way into their body. The exposure and focus of this public act of listening may occasionally promote a profound reaction. The listener may cry or become activated by a very strong emotion such as euphoria or even anger. This is not the goal, but be prepared for what may be triggered and allow the listener space to decide how best they wish to respond to whatever has been experienced. When working with vulnerable groups it may be useful to warn them against choosing anything that has a connection to a very recent, painful or unprocessed experience or memory.

Further outcomes can be developed depending on the nature of the group. You could explore ways in which the exercise could be applied to scenario and character, operating as an extension of Stanislavskian 'emotional memory' work, suggesting possible applications to text and the development of character. At its heart, however, the exercise is a means of revealing the inner word of musicality and how this can be transformed and shaped by the experience of listening to music.

Rhythm as meaning – an introductory exercise

Overview

This exercise is suited to anyone over the age of 15. It is a good starting activity for a group as it contains an element of warm-up. Like the previous exercise it is not too challenging and therefore can be achieved by beginners and groups that are new to one another. It relates to Mithen's notion of 'Hmmmmm', providing an illustration of how musical ideas underpin the way we read and communicate meaning. It also connects to Stanislavski's Method of Physical Action and his ideas about Tempo Rhythm.

Requirements of the exercise

1 A group of six or more people.

2 A room big enough to allow the group to stand in a circle.

The exercise

- The group stand in a circle facing the centre.

- They have to pass a clap around the circle – this is the same starting instruction as a well-known theatre game called *Zip Zap Boing*, but it must not develop into this game and must be played without vocal sound, other than those sounds made as a natural response to the exercise.

- They must make eye contact with the person they are passing the clap to.

- The clap must be passed around the circle in one direction until the group find flow and a sense of shared attention.

- Once this has been achieved you instruct them to send the clap around the circle in the other direction.

- The group is then instructed that they can send the clap in whatever direction they choose. Requiring them to create a sort of conversation between one another as the clap is passed back and forth.

- The group will begin to react, they may laugh when the clap is passed repeatedly between two individuals for example. Ask them what they are reacting to – what you are looking for is recognition that the clap is beginning to take on the characteristics of speech and have meaning – some exchanges may have the feeling of mini-arguments or confrontations, for example.

- Let play continue allowing the group to change direction whenever they choose.

- With the idea of communication now in place, groups will begin to play. The clap will begin to vary in intensity and changes of tempo will emerge as playful relationships begin between individuals.

- In shy or inhibited groups it may be necessary to encourage play – much better, however, if it can be something they discover.

- Again stop and ask for quick comments on how the group is beginning to perceive the clapping:

  a) Does a loud or hard clap feel different from a soft or quiet one?

  b) Do quick exchanges suggest different meaning to slower exchanges?

  c) Do they read ideas such as status, character or relationship from the clapping?

- Following this brief discussion, the exercise continues, but this time they are instructed that the clap can be sent across the circle as well as in either direction.

- By now most groups will begin to experiment with different ideas and emotions. Body language and facial expressions may play a part, but what we are primarily interested in is the way the clap and the rhythm it creates begins to have meaning.

- Once again a brief pause should be offered where the group can talk about what is happening. You may wish to point out moments where meaning was particularly clear or get them to think about both the reception and the experience of clapping. How does it feel to receive a clap that is hard or soft and how does it feel to actually clap in these various ways? The action of clapping will change us as well as those we are clapping at.

- Finally, instruct the group to work within certain musical parameters: a round governed by simple instructions such as 'soft and fast' or 'hard and slow' claps, for example.

- Be strict with them – there is often an instinct to speed up slow tempos or slow down faster ones, which should be resisted.

- Discuss how it felt and what changed in the room.

Outcomes

Once the initial idea is established the group should easily find changes in their inner experience of the exercise. In the latter stages of the exercise, for example, the instruction to work within a slow tempo but with a soft clap, can be very powerful, groups often talk about how tense it feels or frightening, it may suggest ideas of character or dramatic context. What is certain is that the effect is tangible, the room changes and they feel it. They may well talk of the slower speeds feeling calmer, but equally there will be those who find it frustrating and anxious-making. The point here is that tempo suggests meaning, not that given tempi have finite meaning. It is useful to finish the exercise by hinting at applications. What, for example, is the tempo and dynamic quality of a feeling such as jealousy? A young person who has caught their partner snogging someone else, the sort of naturalistic setting we might find in a soap opera, could be fast and light, but what of Othello's jealousy as he enters Desdemona's bed chamber at the top of Act Five, how would we characterize that? This may well help the actor to find emotional starting points that are beyond their own lived experience. The ambition is to remind them that rhythm has meaning and that we can use this to help explore and communicate inner life. The Method of Physical Action is at play during the exercise as we experience the act of clapping at various strengths and speeds promoting meaning as well as communicating it, the manipulation of action using musical instructions in turn offering the actor a mechanism to shape and transform inner experience and emotion.

Music as physical action

These are a series of exercises that can be offered as one-off activities or workshop exercises, but ideally should be used regularly to develop a sensitivity to musicality as part of an experiential training. Many of these exercises have their roots in the practice of Polish theatre company Teatr Piesn Kozla or Song of A Goat Theatre, which was founded by Grzegorz Bral, Anna Zubrzycki and Gabriel Gawin. Bral and Zubrzycki were both members of Gardzienice and much of the work of the company has been informed by this experience and indeed by the ideas of Staniewski. Like Gardzienice the practice and training methodology of Teatr Piesn Kozla seeks to explore the connections between body, voice and music, with the notion of musicality being central to their ethos and aesthetic. The performance work of both companies is distinctive and the result of a training and research based approach to theatre making, which draws inspiration from the laboratory model established by Grotowski, whose studio space in Wroclaw was Teatr Piesn Kozla's first home. Their approach is not obviously compatible with mainstream theatre making and training as it is applied in the psychological realist traditions of the UK and America. As a result their methodologies need to be viewed as a starting point requiring adaptation, as a means of accessing and developing sensitivity to the notion of musicality that can then be applied to text and performance in a range of contexts.

Embodied rhythm

Overview

These exercises exploit the natural physiological and neurological connections between music and movement, encouraging the ability to communicate through and read meaning from rhythm, promoting ensemble sensitivity and tapping into deeper levels of connection between actors. They speak to both the idea of liberating instincts as articulated by Staniewski[7] and Mithen and to the notion of 'impulse' as a means of establishing connection, as applied in the work of Sanford Meisner. The exercises also exploit psychophysical connections as suggested by Stanislavski's Method of Physical Action. They encourage the development and recognition of a key characteristic within musicality, that of 'flow'. Flow, in this context, refers to the way in which rhythmic and by extension musical shape requires a fluidity of expression. The act of establishing a regular rhythm, for example, requires the creation of sound through action, followed by further action, or reaction, required to maintain it. In this sense one could say that the rhythm plays us, as much as we play the rhythm.

Requirements of the exercises

1   Group of six or more people.

2   They are physically demanding and require a room large enough for a group to move around in safely. Participants will need to wear suitable clothing that allows free movement and the exercises are best done in bare feet.

3   The act of stepping in repetitive rhythmic patterns can be very
    tiring and put strain on the knees, ankles and feet. Groups
    get better at this as they progress, but anyone leading this
    work should be mindful of the physical stamina required and
    temper it accordingly.

4   This exercise can vary in length depending on the focus, age
    and level of the group; ideally, however, one should give it at
    least 20 minutes to half an hour.

Preliminary exercise

- The group begins walking freely in the space, finding a tempo
  that feels comfortable and that reflects an inner sense of rhythm.

- They should walk freely and simply around the space, but
  avoid walking in circles, using all the space available.

- The feet are beating out inner tempo and reflecting it back,
  both establishing it and sounding it out.

- Once this has settled the group should be instructed to work
  very specifically with their chosen tempo, giving it a regular
  almost metronomic quality, as if the tempo were now leading
  them.

- There is no need to dance, march or skip, just simply mark
  each step as if it were a beat of a drum, creating a sense of
  fluidity and flow to the walk.

- Once this has been established, get them to open their
  attention to include the room and each other – to play their
  rhythm against that of others.

- You could encourage them to walk in pairs, feeling what it is
  like to hear and play their rhythm against that of a partner.

- Ask them how they receive these various rhythms, what it
  feels like. How do they read the rhythm of others – perhaps
  they can read tempo in the eyes or attitude for example.

- When it feels like the group is ready to move on, instruct them to find a common tempo, with everyone walking very precisely to the same beat, but still freely around the room – we are not looking for marching, but simply a shared pulse.

- Allow them the time it takes to find this shared tempo.

- If in doubt or if a group seems to be disheartened then encourage unity by beating out a rhythm either with your feet, hands or on a drum.

- Once unity is achieved the group should be allowed to enjoy and explore the sensation. They should not be dancing or marching, but something more fluid, interconnected and alive. Their feet working together, but still a sense of polyphony from the bodies.

- Encourage playfulness and instruct the group to allow their breathing to regulate itself, naturally responding to the exercise, creating its own polyrhythm against the shared pulse found in the step.

- The activity is strangely engaging and it is worth being brave enough to let it continue. As they tire they also give up trying to animate the exercise in a superficial or performative way, allowing them to access deeper resonances and connections. It is the repetition that is crucial for this to occur.

- Encourage the exercise into the whole body using the following instructions or ones like them – for more experienced or open groups this may occur without prompts:

    a) Find a simple connection between the ankles and the wrists.

    b) Extend the relationship to the neck and base of the spine: so ankles, wrists, neck and the base of the spine are engaged by the pulse. Not in a dance, but in a playful exploration.

- Encourage them to explore how they receive and react to the rhythm of others.

- The exercise can be extended by getting some to stay still as others continue to work – men, for example, could be asked to stand still whilst the women work around them or vice versa. You might tap individuals on the shoulder and instruct all but those who have been tapped to stand still whilst the others work.

- Those in stillness should stay alive to the pulse, maintaining it as an inner sense even though their bodies are still.

- Once it ceases to be interesting to the group they can return to their original tempos before stopping.

Outcomes

This exercise has a ritualistic feel. Once the shared tempo is created then there can be a powerful drive achieved by the flow of the rhythm of the step which is experienced both through the sound of the feet and in the body. It is important that groups are encouraged to see the exercise as a way of establishing connections, rather than an invitation to explore an internal or ecstatic engagement. This is after all an ensemble acting exercise. The group, if left and encouraged to play, will find the collective power that the shared tempo can offer, promoting and enabling an ensemble sensitivity to establish. The rhythm becomes a conduit for a collective experience.

Follow-up exercise one – establishing a 'rhythm circle'

- Ask the group to walk together until they once again find a collective step and tempo. But this time, once the step is established, they are to accentuate the first of four steps, until a collective and repeated 'four-step' is created. Step one being accented, followed by steps two, three and four. Then the pattern repeated continuously.

- The group work together, using this four-step to move around the room, making sure they use the whole space freely and do not get stuck going around in circles.

- The first accented beat should feel like the impulse or impetus for the next three, as if the accented foot continues to resonate throughout the body creating a sense of fluidity in the movement.

- The tempo should be moderate, to encourage a drive and flow, but not so fast as to tire the group.

- They should not be dancing, but working with the step in a natural way, finding fluidity and freedom, but with a body and breath that responds to the exercise freely without a rigid sense of choreographed movement.

- Once the rhythm is established the group get into a circle facing inward, still maintaining the step.

- In this 'rhythm circle' the step is encouraged to be as precise as it can be. The sensation of a chorus working on a single idea of a collective four-step. They must listen and respond as an ensemble allowing the quality and shape of the step to be discovered or revealed rather than imposed.

- Once the four-step feels robust and precise try changing to a three-step – step one is accented followed by steps two and three. The feet always alternating in a constant flow.

- The group needs to find a collective understanding of each pattern. A shared sense. A feeling of chorus and of mutuality.

- Try shifting from one pattern to the next, without losing flow.

- Once this has been practised and achieved with precision and without loss of flow, instruct the group to alternate the step on a given signal from you. So one person stays with the four-step, while the person next to them changes to a three-step. This pattern is repeated around the circle until the group is evenly divided between those who are going to stay on a four-step and a neighbour who is going to change to a three-step.

- On your instruction the change happens – the 'rhythm-circle' now contains a four-step and a three-step played against each other. The core steps are still in time with one another, but the accents are now different, resulting in a polyphonic texture that is both audible and physicalized.

- Once established instruct the group to clap on the shared accent – every third pattern of the four-step will connect with the fourth set of the three-step, creating a moment when the whole group should be accenting the same step.

- To end it may be helpful to instruct the group to run freely before slowing to a walk and then stopping.

Outcomes

This development offers a stronger sense of chorus, ensemble and mutuality, facilitating an intense sense of rhythmic engagement and embodiment. It is a useful warm-up promoting focus, release and a sense of ensemble, but is also powerful way of developing sensitivity to musicality, the embodying of the rhythm allowing the inner musical landscape to make its way into the body and be read by others. As groups get more confident with this work you can add other steps to the repertoire such as a five-step, which is a three-step followed by a two-step: in flow the step would look like this, with the accented step in bold: **Right**, left, right, **left,** right/**Left,** right, left, **right,** left/ **Right,** left, right, **left,** right. Rhythm circles can also be created using clapping instead of stamping, but the step encourages whole body movement and flow in a much more complete and visceral way.

Follow-up exercise two – rhythm and counter rhythm

Rhythm

- The group find a common rhythmic step, in the way suggested in the preliminary exercise. They are then guided into a four-step and into the formation of a rhythm circle.

- Encourage individuals to come into the centre of the circle and stamp out their own improvised responses to the collective four-step. The group surrounding become a chorus to their protagonist, supporting and helping to shape and drive the ideas, much like a band might support and respond to a soloing instrumentalist.

- The central performance or musical lead will appear like a piece of primitive performance work, with physicalized and released body ideas informing the rhythmic shapes being stamped out through the feet. The steps in this sense become the text with meaning emerging and being reinforced by the group.

- The task should be repeated until everyone in the group has had a go, or until the exercise loses its joy or focus.

Counter rhythm

- This version of the exercise is built up in the same way but instead of working in sympathy with the chorus, the protagonist is required to try to break the rhythm, using it as a provocation, finding physical life and rhythmic steps that cut across or work as a counter rhythm.

- The chorus still work in response, finding ways in which the tension between the rhythms can be used to shape and drive the ideas.

Outcomes

Both these exercises build strong ensemble relationships whilst developing a sensitivity to how we read and use rhythm as communication. They replace text with non-referential rhythmic sound and as a result can have applications in both music-making and text work. The exercises can be used as part of a rehearsal process or as a means of developing character, by asking the actor to explore the essence of their characters or a given moment in the play using the rhythmic steps as the form of communication. This can be done with more than one actor in the circle, allowing for duos or character groups to explore relationships and inner connections.

A ball game

- The group find a shared three-step as outlined in the preliminary exercise.

- Once this is established the ball can be introduced.

- The group have to throw and catch the ball so that it becomes part of the rhythm. To begin with this means throwing on the first beat of the three-step, catching within the flow of the rhythm and then throwing on the first beat of the next cycle of three.

- Be patient, every group will eventually find a way to achieve it.

- The flow of the movement of the ball has to be maintained and followed-through by the catcher, before they throw it to the next person.

- The ball cannot be caught in such a way as the rhythm stops, instead the body must respond to the impulse of the throw, following the energy of the ball in the process of catching, before processing that into the throw. The ball becomes part of the rhythm, as if it were a text or melody being tossed around by the chorus.

- As the exercise develops encourage the group to become more playful, releasing sound and exploring how the ball can be used to develop relationships and explore atmosphere and narrative ideas.

- The exercise should eventually read like an improvised and ever-changing narrative.

Outcomes
This is a good warm-up game that promotes ensemble focus and play. It can be used to explore character and narrative ideas by simply asking the group to work with their characters in mind.

Embodying sound and singing

Overview
The following exercises apply the same core principles of the rhythm work to singing. They offer a means of physicalizing sound and of promoting an understanding of music as action, developing in turn a sense of music as space. They speak to Roesner's ideas of musicality as a way of reading performance space and the visual and physical properties of theatre. They can also be seen as a way of extending the idea of atmosphere as used by Michael Chekov, extending his ideas of how music can be used as a way of reading dramaturgical structure.

Requirements
1 Groups of eight or more people.
2 Can be done by groups who have no previous singing experience[8].

3 Needs a space big enough to enable movement.

4 Work in bare feet and in clothes that allow free movement.

Finding the choral sound: A sensitizing exercise

- The group stand in a circle facing inwards.

- They sing a drone or shared note that sits easily within their range to an 'ah' sound. The note does not need to be within the same octave and so women may sing the note an octave higher than the men and vice-versa, as long as the note is the same.

- Encourage them to find a collective sound, in such a way that they hear the group note rather than their own as the predominant sound, singing only as loudly as is required for this to happen. They should refresh their breath whenever they need to, not worrying about finding a choral moment to breath. The result should be a continuous drone.

- Eventually, and often quite quickly, the group will create a harmonic, which will sound like a ringing overtone, as if the sound is reverberating in the space. This we will call the *crown*, which is the term given to it by a Siberian singing group who taught me this exercise while working with Teatr Piesn Kozla on a production of *Macbeth*.

- Encourage them to hear the *crown* when it is achieved. You might want to circle your finger in the air once it appears so that the group can recognize when they have achieved it.

- The group should be encouraged to sing in such a way as to strengthen the *crown*, becoming a point of focus for the ensemble, tapping into the physical properties of sound waves and moving the group away from aesthetic ideas about singing.

- Explore new drone notes and different sounds such as 'oo' or 'ee', always searching for the *crown* as they do this.

- Divide the group in half, but still in an inward facing circle.

- Re-establish a common drone note and then get one half of the group to sing another note against it. Still searching for the collective sound and the physical sensation of sound vibrating and ringing in the space. You can use any note – what we might class as discordant harmony can be very effective at promoting this sense of physical sound. For example, an interval of a second, which is a note and the next note in the scale sung together (a C and D for instance) can promote a very pronounced and almost unbearable vibration and harmonic ring.

- Play with different intervals, asking members of the group to lead. Always using physical gestures to facilitate and guide the singers and searching for ways of promoting a sense of harmonic ring and vibration between the notes.

- Continue until the group seems to have had enough or time runs out.

Outcomes

This exercise is a means of subverting the usual focus of singing work. It is not about singing in tune, but rather about finding a collective physical sensation through singing which will results in a shared tuning. The sound used to facilitate this process should prioritize the physical properties rather than any measure relating to the aesthetics of the voice. The crown is best achieved without vibrato and as a result the actor is forced to move away from ideas about singing correctly and towards the idea of singing as a visceral activity. In this way it speaks to Mithen's idea of 'Hmmmmm' and creates a sense of sound as physical space and atmosphere.

Singing in 'rhythm circles'

- Establish a four-step as outlined in the embodied rhythm exercises.

- Once established the group are instructed to sing a common note to an 'ah' sound, on the first accented step of each pattern of four. The sound, like the accented step, should be seen as the impetus for the movement, as if they are 'surfing on the sound'. The sung note lasting as long as the step and then resounding on the first beat of the next cycle. As if they are stepping on a platform created by the sound.

- Once this is established walk alongside individuals suggesting new notes and even new rhythmic accents, making sure that the note always sounds on an accented step.

- Repeat this process until you have created a vocal texture of harmonies and polyrhythms that pleases you and is sustainable by the group.

- Encourage the group to move into a rhythm circle, containing all the notes and different rhythmic accents you have installed, united by a common beat of the feet.

- Encourage them to find a way of developing a collective sound, informed by both their physical life and singing. This is drawing on sensitivities built up in the earlier exercises, but now bringing sung and physicalized rhythmic shape together.

- Try applying different dynamic instructions to the sound, always indicated through physical gesture, rather than vocal instruction: softer, louder, faster, slower.

- You could encourage individuals into the centre to improvise sung melody against the sound, mirroring the protagonist, chorus work done in the rhythm exercises.

- The exercise stops once the group has had enough or a natural musical end is achieved.

Outcomes

This offers a means of uniting physical action and singing, encouraging a sense of music as physical action. The movement around the room, whilst singing, also strengthens the idea of sound as three-dimensional space: once in the 'rhythm circle' the choral sound creates an active space that can then be inhabited by the protagonist. It enables the group to find ways of connecting through singing and of reawakening the idea of music as communication. The actor-musician is able to experience how music-making can change and connect to inner life and how musical choices can both shape and be shaped by the work of others, a very useful starting point for the development of integrated music-making and a key sensitivity required when working with music as underscore or as an integrated element of storytelling.

Human logic: Connections between singing, space and language

Overview

This exercise gets its name from the music software Logic, which enables the user to create loops and overlapping tracks. It also reminds us of the implied hierarchy in communication, which sees musical qualities subjugated by the semantic values of language. Here musical sound is given prominence. The exercise is based on the idea of building layers of *ostinato* sung figures or loops. Once again musical instructions should be reinforced by the use of physical gesture, encouraging the group to perceive the sound as having physical properties, the layers becoming structures that the group are constructing in space as well as in sound. As if they were creating a set as much as a piece of music.

Preliminary exercise

- The group stand in an inward facing circle.

- A leader or conductor is chosen from the group

- The leader has to get the group to sing a musical figure. This may be a drone or rhythmic motif, what is important is that it is improvised; they should not be teaching an existing song or something they know.

- Once the first pattern is established by the whole group, they then pick a sub group, perhaps two or three people standing together within the circle and get them to create a second musical figure or loop that fits over the first.

- This process is then repeated until they are satisfied with the collective sound.

- The facilitator can remove or mute parts in order to create variation and structure.

- Each piece should continue for as long as it remains of interest. The facilitator is responsible for finding an ending for the composition, either by cutting the group off or diminuendo to a finish or perhaps removing parts until the piece feels like it can stop.

Outcomes

The exercise encourages basic compositional skills and ensemble music-making. It builds on earlier exercises by increasing the sensation of sung sound as having three-dimensional qualities: a place and atmosphere as much as a sound. It encourages the group to develop and change their music-making in response to the emerging composition. A given part or loop, has a very different feel once it is contextualized by the next layer: this search for musical identity and a collective understanding is part of the exercise and should be encouraged and even discussed.

Follow-up exercise one

Overview

The exercise follows the same shape as before but this time a context is provided by trigger words. The words become provocations for the compositions and can be made-up or generated in response to a project or play being rehearsed. An example might be words such as: man, woman, love, God, peace, death, boredom, hunger.

The exercise

- The group stand in an inward facing circle.

- The member who elects to lead is given one of the trigger words, written on a scrap of paper: they must not reveal it to the group at this stage.

- They then create a musical structure using the techniques outlined above, in response to the word.

- Once the musical shape has been established the word is shown to the group, as they are singing. This will lead to a shift in the quality of the singing as the context it provides begins to reverberate and act on the music.

- Once you have found an ending it may be worth pausing for a moment to discuss how the word changed the singing and informed the music, before repeating the exercise with a new leader and a fresh word.

Outcomes

This is a very simple way of demonstrating how language and music are interrelated, how one can inform the other. What is important here is that the group begin to make the music without knowledge of the trigger word. This prioritizing of the musical experience is an important reminder of how we can create deep and textured meaning from musical processes which can then inform our understanding of words. It also offers an interesting way of expressing ideas, as it asks the facilitator to explain their understanding of a word or idea in music.

Follow-up exercise two – exploring text

- This version follows exactly the same process as above but this time is connected to a given text or poem that the group is working on.

- The facilitator choses a word from the text that they feel reveals something about the piece or that is intriguing or important to them.

- They then use this word as the starting point for the exercise, but taking care not to reveal it.

- Once the sound is established the word is shared with the group.

- If the group is ready you can then ask the facilitator to speak the poem or speech, using the music they created as underscore. Like the earlier 'rhythm circles' the chorus must respond to the protagonist and the text, searching for ways in which the music can support, drive and react to the action in the centre.

- Encourage the group to listen to the text and not overpower it – to support and be guided by it and by the performer, rather than pushing or leading them.

Outcomes
In many ways this is the pinnacle of the sensitivity work. The music is an underscore but also a setting for the central performance. A sound world that supports and reflects its content and the inner life of the actor presenting it, but that also provides a space and atmosphere for it to exist within. In this way it replicates Michael Chekov's idea about

atmosphere. The exercise is very important for actor-musicians to explore how music can inform inner life and how music can operate alongside text as a development of meaning – like Mithen's ideas it reminds us that music is part of communication. The text is often pushed into flow and musical shape in a way not imaginable without the music and in turn even the most simple of musical textures can become complex and multi-layered as the spoken text provides meaning and context. It promotes a deep connection to the words in the speaker and offers a means of exploring dramaturgical and vocal shape, as the musical landscape echoes and encourages shifts in the voice, body and text.

Follow-up exercise three – adding instruments

Overview
Once sensitivity and connection have been promoted using singing and physical movement you can begin to add musical instruments to the work. The ambition is that the group simply extend their discoveries into the instruments, rather than abandon the focus and start setting up for a band rehearsal. The group should start in the inward facing circle with the instruments added only one at a time.

The exercise
- The facilitator works in the same way as above
- A musical texture is created with loops that include sung sound and instrumental sound
- The instrumentalists should be encouraged to play by the facilitator using the same vocabulary used for singing. This may need to be a more collaborative process as players unused to working without music may have to adapt the idea sung to them. The ambition remains the same: to create a musical texture constructed of loops or *ostinato* phrases.

- As the exercise is repeated so more instruments can be added.

- It may be useful to subvert the exercise structure and start with a solo instrument – a drum, for example, could lead the work.

Outcomes

We have now moved from sound made by the body into instrumental sound, but in such a way that it should feel like an extension of the voice and body, that builds on the sensitivities established in earlier exercises. As with earlier versions the music should be felt as well as heard – the circle filled with the sound creating a sense of atmosphere and space. The physical presence of the instruments is at this stage simply incidental and not to be considered – if an instrument requires someone to sit then that is fine, just make sure they are included in the circle and that they can still make contact with the group.

Accidental chords

Overview

This last exercise can be done with voices and instruments or a combination of both. It is based on a simple idea. The facilitator conducts the ensemble to create improvised chords. The notes should be chosen at random by the individuals in the group and the sum total of their collective sound left to find its own shape and feel.

The exercise

- The group stand in an inward facing circle
- A facilitator is chosen to conduct the exercise
- The group must choose a note which they sound on a signal from the conductor or facilitator

- There are many ways to lead, but to begin with they may wish to count in, with the group playing or singing their improvised or accidental chord on the fourth beat.

- The conductor explores ways to bring them in at varying intensities and volume and cut them off.

- Start with a series of separated chords until the exercise is established, progressing into a series of chords that follow one from the other. The idea is to try to create a musical structure that has some sort of logical progression.

- Find ways of creating crescendos and moments of diminuendo, all informed by the emerging music.

- Each chord will have its own unpredictable sound and feel, requiring the conductor to adapt and find a way of shaping and moving forward.

- The exercise can also be used to create an underscore for text. The text is spoken in the centre of the circle, the conductor responsible for leading a series of accidental chords in response.

Outcomes

Once again the exercise encourages us to find meaning and dramatic shape in music. The accidental nature of the chords is part of its strength, forcing the leader and the group to find collective meaning. It is playful and once again helps to build ensemble sensitivity as well as musicality. It can also be used as a starting point for devised music and text – with stories being written in response to the found shapes and atmospheres or melodies written to this random but often rather beautiful harmonic structure.

Applying musicality to performance

These exercises are offered as training methods, but they can also be applied and adapted to devising and rehearsal processes. They offer a means of developing the sensitivity to musicality explored in the previous section for use in the development of acting skills or processes such as the building of character, emotional or inner life and supporting dramaturgical shape. They are ideal for actor-musicians who may be required to extend their attention into the playing of music as an integrated element of performance, but can equally be used with actors who do not play. Some exercises rely on the playing of instruments, but in most cases this can be substituted by singing or indeed simple music-making achievable by most actors. They are in this sense an exploration of the musicality of performance.

Rhythm and tempo

Overview
This collection of exercises builds on the sensitizing work outlined in the rhythm exercises. They all speak broadly to Stanislavski's idea of Tempo Rhythm, and indeed have been inspired by that idea, exploiting the same connection between rhythm, inner life, physicality and text.

Inner and outer rhythm

Requirements
1 The exercise can be done by a small group or even indviduals, but will also work with larger groups.

2 The exercise is moderately physical but does not require movement clothing.

3 It is suitable for most groups including those new to acting.

The exercise

- Instruct the group to walk around the room freely, using the whole space and avoiding getting stuck in circles.

- As in the preliminary rhythm exercise, they are to find a tempo that reflects how they feel at that moment. Both reflecting and establishing a sense of inner tempo.

- Once this is established the group are asked to walk 10 per cent faster, using the whole space and maintaining awareness so that they do not bump into one another. They inhabit this new outer tempo with an inner tempo that enables them to 'own' their physicality.

- Once this has established you ask them to walk 10 per cent faster still. Again they must own this new tempo and think about how it is changing them and their perception of the room and of one another.

- The instruction is repeated until they are going as fast as they can without running. Always the tempo is to be inhabited creating unity between inner and outer experience.

- They are then instructed to go back to their original speed, their comfortable natural tempo. While walking at this speed you can ask them to think about what just happened and how it affected them or their perception of the room and each other.

- The exercise is now reversed.

- Instruct them to walk 10 per cent slower. Inhabiting the tempo and exploring how it changes them. Repeating the instruction until the group are walking so slowly that movement is barely occurring. It is hard to inhabit these very slow tempos, so keep encouraging them. Your teaching style and way of communicating must echo and support the tempo of the exercise.

- Ask them to return to their starting tempo and use this chance to encourage them to consider what they just felt and experienced.

- The exercise is then continued, but this time you ask them to speed their inner tempo up by 10 per cent but without allowing the body to follow. Their walk remains the same or perhaps even slows down, while their inner tempo increases.

- Again you build this in increments until they are exploring a very fast inner tempo while the body is walking slowly or perhaps even standing still.

- Once the ideas has been given time to establish you return to the comfortable or natural tempo and encourage some brief reflection as they walk.

- Now the exercise is reversed – 10 per cent slower inner tempo, but the body remaining the same or perhaps speeding up. Culminating in them walking as fast as they can but with their inner tempo as slow as they can make it.

- They return to the starting tempo before stopping to discuss.

Outcomes

The first phase of the exercise establishes that inner and outer tempo can be separated and that the juxtaposition of the two can suggest very particular emotional states, narrative situations and other manifestations of inner and imaginative life. It builds on ideas of rhythm and meaning explored in the musicality work. It is also interesting for them to observe and consider how inner tempo is felt and experienced in others. You can see it in people's eyes and 'feel' it coming from them. A reminder of just how nuanced our relationship to musical meaning is and how it still informs our understanding of one another.

Follow-on exercise

- The group is instructed to consider a character they are playing or a speech that they are working on.

- They must explore a speech or moment in the play using the relationship between inner and outer tempo as the governing factor.

- The exercise should begin with a physical exploration with the text being gradually added, first as a whisper and then in full voice.

- Encourage them to play and explore various combinations until they find something that fits or feels right.

- Their bodies simply reflect and strengthen the sense of inner and outer tempo, but should eventually be encouraged into character based action – for some this may mean that the speech is spoken as they run or walk around the space, for others they may find physical stillness but with a shifting inner rhythm and tempo.

- Once the idea has established you may want to suggest that some of the speeches are shared with the group.

Outcomes

The exercise encourages new discoveries and deeper connections to text and character, by prioritizing the underlying rhythmic structures that can underpin emotion and textual or narrative meaning. It is a good way of moving into text and performance work while maintaining a musical framing. It is a task that draws on musicality as a means of working with emotional truth and dramaturgical form without subverting it stylistically.

Musicality and objectives

Overview

This exercise uses the Stanislavskian notion of objectives as a governing force for action and the promotion of inner life. It is an extension of the tempo rhythm work outlined above that can be done by most groups of actors regardless of level or age.

Requirements

- Groups or individuals can attempt this exercise, although it is best done with others to facilitate discussion and offer a point of focus.
- The exercise can be achieved in any space and requires no instruments.

The exercise

- The group is asked to fulfil a simple physical action of their choosing. They may walk across the room and sit down, or stand up and move to the window. This is done without a narrative context.
- They must then choose a simple rhythmic and musical instruction which they use to shape the action: do it faster or slower, more lyrically or in a staccato fashion.
- How does this inform the action? What meaning does it suggest?
- Now they must develop the idea by giving it a context and objective that governs the action. They might be moving to the window to see if someone they love is returning home, or sitting down to stop themselves from fainting. The objective does not have to be complex, but just enough to offer a stronger framing for the action.

- Explore the action, asking how the objective has changed the tempo, rhythm or quality.

- Once again they are instructed to apply musical instructions to the action. This can now become more specific: what happens, for example, if the physical action is divided into sections that each have a different musical quality or tempo? What does this do to their understanding of the action and how does it affect or colour their relationship to the objective?

- You might then share some of these with the group.

Outcome

The exercise reveals the complex ways in which rhythm and tempo can both promote and communicate meaning. There is a correlation here to the introductory rhythm exercise: we find that musical form helps to colour objectives and other semantic ideas, and rather than imposing a meaning they augment and interact with ideas, offering new textures and awakening previously unconsidered inner responses. It offers potential ways of understanding and developing music to accompany physical action, highlighting how much meaning can be altered by musicality.

Follow-on exercise

- A physical action is developed and a governing objection decided, either invented or taken from an actual scenario.

- Music is then played as the action is performed. The music both colours reception of the action and can be used to inform the action.

- Try exploring both these ideas.

- One time the actor ignores the music, leaving only the audience to find the meaning revealed by the co-existence of music and action. Then instruct the actor to allow their work to be informed by what the music suggests.

- You can then use live instruments to develop the exercise.
- Begin to interrogate how musical content and instrumentation alter and inform both process and reception.

Outcomes

This offers a simple way to explore how music can be used as an integrated part of acting processes. It reveals the impact music has on meaning for both performer and audience – so often the emphasis of music-making in theatre is on how the music informs audience reception and yet here the music is being opened up to the actor as part of the process of creating and making choices.

iPod impros

Overview

This is a collection of exercises that use pre-recorded music. They exploit the fact that most young people and many adults have access to hundreds and often thousands of recordings on their smartphones or MP3 players and are suitable for non-instrumentalists as well as a starting point for actor-musicians. They connect to Blacking's ideas about musical specialism, reminding us that we all possess musicality and that the process of listening and responding to music is also a musical action.

Requirements

1 Can be done with any group 15 years and over.
2 Each participant will need to bring a music player, a selection of music and headphones.

3 You will need speakers or a sound system with suitable connecting cables.

Personal anthems

- As with our first musicality exercise, each member of the group is asked to bring a piece of music that means something to them and that connects to a personal memory or moment in their lives.

- A volunteer agrees to play their musical choice as the rest of the group watches and listens. There should be enough space between them to create a basic audience performer relationship.

- The music is played on speakers so that everyone can hear it.

- First the music is played without giving a context – the group are then asked what they think the story or memory might be, based on both the music and their observations of the listener.

- The volunteer then tells his or her story.

- We then listen to the music again, followed by a discussion of what changed in our reception of the story, the person and their music.

- The exercise is then repeated with a new volunteer, but this time they are asked to tell the story while the music is playing. They can choose when to speak and must use the music as a framing device for the story telling, the event lasting as long, but no longer than, the music dictates. You may wish to control the volume of the music as the exercise progresses.

- The group watch and listen, before discussing what they saw and heard.

Follow-on suggestions

1   The exercise can be repeated in various permutations: the
    story can be told after, before or during the music, helping to
    highlight the various ways that we use music to colour and
    define meaning.

2   Once a few members of the group have had a turn, an
    interesting variation is to mix stories and musical choices.
    So a story is told using another person's music: this could
    be led by you or just chosen at random. An example that
    springs to mind is when a student shared a memory of their
    grandmother, but we used the music from an earlier story
    about a teenage party as underscore. Our understanding of
    the story and of the grandmother was completely changed
    and the storyteller was forced to find new textures and
    performance choices in response.

3   The group can be asked to create tableaus after hearing the
    story. The music is then played and the tableaus activated.
    An example I recall was when a group worked on a memory
    of a holiday road-trip. The tableaus depicted various modes
    of transport and a few moments involving the storyteller and
    his girlfriend, who got together during the trip. The musical
    choice was extremely spirited and when played loudly it led
    to a wonderfully playful activation of the group, including
    a car crash and the couple dancing under imagined stars.
    The music released the imagery and inner life, offering an
    impulse for movement and interrelation that was governed
    by their knowledge of the story. A lovely way to encourage
    playful improvisation and make discoveries about character,
    physicality and inner life, which could be applied to a text or
    devising process.

4   You could ask them to bring in objects relating to their story,
    which can then be shared using the music as underscore. An

example that was particularly affecting was when a student brought in a fur coat that had belonged to her grandmother. She told the story relating to the coat in silence. The group then very simply took turns to put the coat on as the music played. The result was strangely compelling as a piece of performance, but was also a reminder of Stanislavskian exercises relating to endowment, the music offering a means of honouring the memory and informing the way the coat was handled and worn. The music in that respect was enabling an interaction between the story and the physical action.

5   The group can also be encouraged to build a simply installation using objects and materials that relate to their story. The music can then be played as the group are encouraged to explore the installation. The story can be shared or the event just left to be interpreted in any way the group decide. What is interesting is just how complete the experience feels once the music is added.

Outcomes

This exercise and its various permutations offer a means to explore and illustrate the complex ways in which music implies and communicates meaning. At the heart of all of them is the fact that music is non-referential and as a result our understanding of it is completely altered by the performance context. Whether an object, a tableau, a story or a physical action, music changes the way we receive and engage as both audience and performer. It can shape the choices we make and help to colour meaning.

Musical endowment

- A chair is placed in the centre of the room.
- The group are all asked to choose a piece of high-energy

music and a contrasting piece of low energy from their collection.

- The group then sit facing the chair, forming an audience.

- One at a time they have to enter the space and sit on the chair. Their relationship to the chair governed completely by the musical choice.

- The action is repeated so that both pieces of music can be used.

- To begin with this is best done with headphones, which intensifies the experience for the actor, but also means that the audience can see how the relationship to the chair changes and indeed how this change is communicated.

Follow-on suggestions

1   The exercise is repeated with the music played through speakers. With the audience now sharing the same sound experience the work often becomes more comedic, encouraging a different audience-actor relationship. Whatever the outcome the differences between the two versions of the exercise are interesting to discuss.

2   The object can of course be changed. Opening a box or chest, for example, can be a very effective choice. The music could also be chosen by the facilitator to enable particular acting choices to be explored. As suggested in the Personal Anthem exercise it can even be used to endow items of clothing or other personal items, such as jewellery or maybe a weapon.

3   Instead of a chair or other object, an actor can be placed in the space and the music used to colour the interaction. This can be done both using headphones and with music played out loud.

4   The exercise can also be done using live music. It is interesting in this version to explore not only how different types of music affect the choice, but also what different instruments offer in terms of meaning and atmosphere.

Outcomes

The exercise is very useful for inexperienced or younger actors: the use of headphones is a good way of overcoming inhibitions, the actor's inner experience is heightened and although they are working in front of an audience they feel less exposed. The same is also true when the music is played through speakers to a lesser extent. The exercise exploits the fact that we are so used to hearing music as underscore, in television, film and computer games, but also in real life, so many people live to a constant soundtrack of their own making as they travel on buses or walk through town wearing headsets. The music gives permission for the imagination to interact and inform engagement with the outside world. You can manipulate the work by choosing music that helps achieve certain outcomes. A particular atmosphere or even an emotional state can be suggested and encouraged. For young and inexperienced actors this can be particularly useful, encouraging them to try things that they might otherwise be inhibited to try.

The musical bus stop

- This exercise is an adaptation of the rather hackneyed improvisation game that asks a pair of actors to play characters waiting at a bus stop.

- Instead of picking characters at random, each one is asked to choose or is given a piece of music to listen to in their headphones. It is useful to begin with if the music is contrasting. A good starting point might be two characters, one with fast music playing, the other with slow.

- The actors are instructed to let the music govern their experience of the exercise.

- The exercise is played out in front of the rest of the group.

- The use of headphones means that the use of language is not possible, but physicality and the exchange of looks is still possible.

- The exercise can then be developed by swapping the music.

- The exercise can of course be used for other settings and as a devising or rehearsal tool.

- The exercise can then be repeated without music, but with the instruction that the actor must hold onto and develop the ideas that they found with the music.

Outcomes

This is a useful way of seeing how inner tempo is communicated and how it can be received by both the audience and other actors. It is again a good exercise to use with young or inexperienced actors as the headphones free them to make discoveries and share choices.

Music as story

- The group are instructed to choose a piece of music that inspires them – not in the aspirational sense, but rather music that inspires imagination, emotion or inner life.

- They then gift their music to another person in the group.

- Each member of the group then listens to the music they have been given on headphones – it may be better if they use their own headphones to avoid ear infections.

- Using a pen and paper they are asked to write down answers to a series of trigger questions that help them extend the listening experience. Questions might include: what temperature does the music suggest? What country? What weather system? What colour? What type of building or landscape? What smell does the music conjure? etc.

- They are then asked to listen to the music again and to write a stream of consciousness in response. They must start writing when the music starts and not stop until it stops.

- The text they have written is then used to create a short piece of theatre.

- They are instructed to work with the headphones on and always in response to the music. They can choose where they work and how they share the story, but they must practise and develop the text in response to the music until it can be performed.

- They then perform the text with the music still playing in headphones throughout, to the person who gifted them the music, as an intimate one-man show.

- The exercise can then be repeated without the music.

Outcomes

This is a useful devising tool, but also a way of deepening connections between music and dramatic narrative. The use of headphones again intensifies the experience for the actor allowing the music to govern the choices and performance. Removing the music is a helpful way of encouraging development as the memory of the music helps to sustain inner life, imagery and emotional connection. The results are usually tangible in the voice and physical life of the actor as well as in this heightened level of connection.

Shared musical stories

- A piece of evocative and atmospheric music is chosen either by the group or the facilitator.

- An actor is chosen to sit or stand in front of the rest of the group who form an audience.

- With headphones on the actor is instructed to listen to the music, but to address the audience in front of them speaking in the first person, present tense. As the music plays they present an improvised monologue shaped and informed by what they hear, perhaps starting by telling us where they are, what they can see and who is with them.

- For experienced groups or those who have done a lot of musicality training the exercise will work without prompts, but it may be helpful to start by getting the group to answer a few trigger questions while listening to the music to encourage imaginative response and offer a context for the improvisation.

- The exercise can then be repeated by another actor from the group who is asked to speak as someone suggested in the original monologue, again with the headphones on and listening to the same piece of music. An example that springs to mind is when a student created a monologue in response to a haunting piece of choral music by Hildegard Von Bingen. She described waiting on a cliff top looking out to sea as her husband sailed off in a ship, her young son standing beside her. The next volunteer had to tell the story from the boy's perspective, again governed by the same music, and finally a third told what the father saw as he looked back from the ship. The three then stood in tableau as we played the music through the speakers.

Outcomes

A deepening of the creative and imaginative potential offered by music, and a suggestion of a devising method. This exercise also encourages actors to improvise and work in the moment. For actor-musicians it offers a chance to explore how music informs meaning and suggests context and atmosphere, something that can be applied in musical performance and composition work.

Opening a text using music

- This exercise is used to open up a piece of extant text. This could be a poem or any dramatic text, but it is particularly useful for working on Shakespeare with young people.

- The text is read by the group in a way that encourages an ensemble aesthetic. You might go round the circle with each person reading a line or reading up until a full stop before swapping.

- The text can then be briefly discussed.

- You then ask the group to choose pieces of music from their collection that they think encapsulate or resonate with the text. They cannot be wrong – it is just their choice, their instinct for what music might go with or speak to the text.

- In the case of Shakespeare it might be that this is done with a particular image or line in mind: what piece of music, for example, would suggest a 'muse of fire'?

- The music is then played and the speech or line is explored in a way that is governed and shaped by the music.

- You may need to encourage the group to go with the flow of the music or you may choose to allow just one member of the group to read, perhaps using a microphone if that is possible.

- The exercise can be repeated using other musical choices
  – each version deepening the collective understanding and
  suggesting new meanings and approaches to performance.

Outcomes

This is a particularly interesting exercise in my experience. For young
people it offers a way of discussing text that avoids the pitfalls of
using language. Those who may shy away from offering opinions in
discussion will often feel capable of offering a musical idea. Young
people like to share their music and this is a way of getting them to
communicate and engage with text. The results are often rich and
always interesting. I can recall a group of inner-city teenagers working
on the Chorus speech from *Henry V*. The language at first was an
obstacle, but using music we broke down the key images, until we
were able to create an ensemble performance using a gritty, urban
dance track of their choosing. Their musical choices unlocked new
and interesting ideas and resonances, it was their version and this
was important. Having their music validated brought them closer
to the text and enabled them to feel they had a voice as well as
unlocking and suggesting performance.

Working with instruments

Overview

Many of the exercises above include the use of instruments. In
the others live music-making can replace the recorded music and
attention can be given to how the playing is shaped by the performance work. This section, however, is aimed at exploring the
dramaturgical impact of bringing instruments into the space and how
the actor-musician can be encouraged to see the instrument as part
of their dramatic expression and as a starting point for acting choices.

Requirements

1　The group must all have an instrument with them, although the standard of musicianship required can vary.

2　The exercises work best if done in a good sized and uncluttered rehearsal space.

The instrument as character

- Each actor-musician chooses a place in the room to put their instrument. The instrument should be safe and able to be left without being held.

- In silence the group are then encouraged to examine their instrument in detail.

- Encourage them to look at it closely. Touch it. Smell it. They can even explore the sound it makes, but not from a place of expertise. What if they had never seen the instrument before? What does a violin sound like if you tap it, for example? Or a trumpet, if you just press the valves?

- This should be done in silence and for a significant amount of time. Long enough for the instruments to be seen through fresh eyes.

- During this process the group must answer a series of questions about the instrument such as: what temperature does the instrument like or suggest? If it were a plant what plant would it be? Does it have a name? What country does it come from? If you ate it what would it taste of? What is its favourite colour? Where would it live? How would you cook it? etc.

- Once this is completed, the group are asked to write a message informed by the trigger questions, written in the first person, present tense. The message is to a stranger and from the instrument. Perhaps it is a message in a bottle.

- Once completed the message is secreted in the instrument, somewhere where it might be found.

- The group then move out of the space and look back at the room that is now inhabited solely by the instruments scattered around on the floor, against walls or on chairs. It is a set or installation. Each instrument is already alive with possibility and energy. The room full of latent potential.

- The group can then respectfully and carefully explore the space, reading the letters before replacing them where they found them, waiting for the next person.

- Discuss.

Follow-on exercises

1 Encourage the group to choose an instrument they are drawn to. One at a time, they read the text of the message in relation to the instrument, with the instrument played as an underscore. The actor-musician player is instructed to play in response to the text; it can be very simple music, the text is after all the main event here. This can then be shaped or reworked as physical possibilities begin to suggest themselves. It can often feel more like a dialogue than monologue.

2 The same process can be applied to speeches, monologues or poems. The actor is allowed to choose an instrument that they think relate or resonate with their text. They then work with that instrument, finding ways in which it can be used as a partner to the text both physically and in terms of musical underscore.

3 If the instrument allows then the actor-musician can work with their own instrument creating a one-man piece using the text and instrument.

4 You can put pairings of instruments together and use the texts as a starting point for creating a duologue or duet, using music, text and physicality suggested by the instrument.

Overview

This exercise considers the instrument as character, its presence and very particular personality is explored by the actor-musician. The impact of the instruments in the space should not be under-estimated, it is important to acknowledge and experience the power and potential they have as both objects and characters. Ultimately the exercise redresses the imbalance that so often governs rehearsal processes: the hierarchy that places text and actor at the top of the creative agenda is subverted, asking us to recognize instead the instrument on its own terms. The follow-on activities rely on the sensitivities developed in the musicality training to facilitate a dialogue between the music and text, the physical dimensions of the relationship should not be ignored, with solutions sought for how the text and performance can contain the playing of the instrument as well as its sound.

Instrument as physicality

- The actor-musicians should work in pairs.

- One plays their instrument while the other observes carefully.

- The partner then begins to mime the playing style, as the other plays.

- Together they work to find the caricature or archetype suggested by the physical act of playing.

- The instrumentalist learning from their partner about how the instrument changes their body shape, using this as a means of extending into clown or archetype, a hybrid physicality that is part human, part instrument.

- The exercise can then be repeated focusing on specific areas of the body or ideas suggested in the playing of the instrument.

Outcome:

This exercise results in a bold physical choice, which can of course be used directly in performance. It also, however, enables the actor-musician to consider how the act of playing can shape their physicality and suggest possibilities for character.

My instrument has a secret

- The actor-musician is asked to consider their instrument in the way suggested in the 'Instrument as Character' exercise. As part of the work they have to decide on a secret that their instrument is keeping from the audience. Perhaps it can fly or maybe one of the strings is ticklish.

- The actor-musician has then to perform a piece of music on their instrument, during which the secret is revealed.

- The more playful choices are often the most useful starting point, but the exercise can be developed to include ideas with more emotionally weight. Perhaps the instrument is dying or in love.

Outcomes

The exercise places the psychological or emotional focus in the instrument, but inevitably in performance it is the actor-musician who has to give this expression. The result is an activity which encourages connection between the two processes, uniting the playing of the instrument with meaning and emotional life.

Musical intention

- This exercise can be used when ensembles of actor-musicians are required to underscore text or accompany singers.

- In many performance contexts actor-musicians are required to play in separate band areas or behind the action or singer; in order to promote a connection with the instruments, this exercise should be done using an inward facing circle.

- Place the protagonist or singer in the centre of the circle. The instrumentalists are then asked to play, but with close attention to the singer or text. They should use the techniques of the 'rhythm circle' to explore ways in which their musical actions and sounds can inform and respond to the physicality, text and/or lyric.

- The actor in the centre in turn can use the experience to find ways of connecting to the music and the other actor-musicians as a chorus.

- The exercise can be repeated until discoveries or strong connections are estabished and sustained.

- The circle is then gradually expanded until the connections and interaction can be preserved even at a distance.

Outcomes
The close proximity and choral focus that the circle enables is important for generating mutuality and interconnection. The goal here is to foster a dialogue between the music and the protagonist, to enable a synergy. The repetition of the song is also important for these connections to be found. This is often lost in processes that follow the traditional models applied to musical theatre, where band and singer are kept apart. The exercise offers a vocal challenge to the performer and it is important that sensitivity is applied in the music-making. The

protagonist must not try to top the band – a microphone may be helpful if the musical forces are large.

Notes

1   Roesner, D., 'Musicality as a Paradigm for the Theatre: A Kind of Manifesto', *Studies in Musical Theatre* 4 (3) (2010): 293–4, doi: 10.1386/smt.4.3.293_1.

2   Staniewski, W. with Hodge, A., ed., *Hidden Territories: The Theatre of Gardzienice* (London and New York: Routledge, 2004), 64.

3   Mithen, S., *The Singing Neanderthals: The Origins of Music, Language, Mind and Body* (London: Phoenix, 2005), 274.

4   Perry, N. *The Universal Language of Lullabies*, BBC World Service 21 January 2013: http://www.bbc.co.uk/news/magazine-21035103 (accessed 5 December 2014).

5   Blacking, J., *A Commonsense view of all music* (Cambridge: Cambridge University Press, 1987), 60.

6   Storr, A., *Music and the Mind* (London: Harper Collins, 1997 [First published 1992]), 26.

7   See note 2.

8   Only a very small percentage of people are genuinely tone-deaf and cannot distinguish pitch. For most people the term simply refers to the fact that they are not in the habit of singing and so need encouragement and practice to find the same note as the rest of the group. If this is the case then the individual should be guided sensitively until they join the group. Always keep the whole group singing the drone note while you do this. Use physical gesture reinforced with gentle singing into the ear to help find the correct pitch. When they join the rest of the group they will *feel* it – use teaching mechanisms that foster a sense of sung sound as a physical phenomenon, use your hand to suggest pitch, raising it higher if the note needs to go up and lower if it needs to fall.

4
DIRECTING ACTOR-MUSICIANSHIP

As directors we are such whores, we want tricks, we want things to inspire us and to inspire the audience in telling the story. For me actor-musicianship is just another toy to play with, another way of whoring.

NIKOLAI FOSTER

In this chapter we will look at how directors approach working with actor-musicians. Actor-musicians, as we have established, can be found in many performance contexts, from children's theatre to commercial musicals, with each context suggesting its own approach. For the purposes of this chapter, however, we will focus on work that uses actor-musicianship as its main aesthetic and conceptual framing, examining the impact this choice has on the process of directing, from casting, design and the selection of material, through to the very particular demands of working with actors who play instruments. Our examination focuses on professional practice rather than theoretical perspectives and includes contributions from leading directors who specialize in actor-musicianship including John Doyle, Bob Carlton, Peter Rowe, Paddy Cunneen and Nikolai Foster. As with all theatre practice it is neither appropriate nor possible to create a set of rules that applies to every production; the chapter is instead a discussion of some of the core sensitivities and considerations that directors working with actor-musicians might need to bear in mind. It is in that sense a provocation rather than a how-to guide. There are of course moments of divergence and contradiction, but let us begin with an area common to all who have contributed to the chapter.

Imagining together

> In Noh Theatre the phrase they use all the time is that the performer and the audience 'imagine together' and I think that is what music does to a piece of theatre. It says that you are going to have to up our game here, because although you live in a world of toasters and toilets not working and buses running late, you are now entering this world where the soul and psyche burst forward into moments of huge poetry. (Paddy Cunneen)

The starting point for all the theatre makers included in this chapter is the imaginative release that actor-musicianship offers them and their audiences. Like all forms of music theatre it has at its core a theatrical or poetic sensibility that director, performer and audience have to reach for collectively. For Paddy Cunneen this act of shared imagining connects to ideas found in Japanese Noh Theatre, the instruments, he suggests, like the masks worn by Noh performers, become the conduit for the imagination, facilitating a flight of fancy and a very particular suspension of disbelief. The presence of the instruments demands a new language from the director, a language that, like music itself, is open and non-referential, that both shapes and is shaped by its performance or narrative context. It is this challenge that John Doyle encourages those approaching actor-musicianship for the first time to accept and open their imaginations to:

> I talk to them about how the use of the instrument can free the imagination, how the use of the instrument challenges the notion of what is right or wrong in theatre making or that there is a

right or wrong. It asks you to look at what realism means in the theatre; those dreaded words realism and naturalism, how do you approach those notions when you have an instrument between your legs? What it invites you to think about is how the use of the instrument or the multi-skilled element of the work asks the audience to engage its own imagination, because without the audience taking the imaginative leap to go beyond the instrument or to allow the instrument to take them to a place that they would never have otherwise been, it would seem ridiculous. That to me is the power of actor-musicianship. The image from *Sweeney Todd* of a girl sitting on top of coffin playing a cello, for example, would never be seen in real life, but it is an image that is potent. Actor-musicianship offers the chance to image-make and stimulate that part of the imagination in the audience that is otherwise untapped.

Doyle goes on to connect this open approach to more fundamental ideas about the function of theatre:

Having the instruments on stage is really a means to an end, that's not for me what the work is about. As a theatre maker one's responsibility is to leave a lot of questions in the room, whether that is the rehearsal room or the theatre. Packaging it into a series of answered questions is unfulfilling for all concerned, which means inevitably that as the artist who is taking the lead in that process, you too end up with a lot of unanswered questions.

A change of emphasis

There are lots of practical considerations that affect the directing, casting and design process and musical arrangements: you are looking for a particular range of instruments, you are thinking about who might be available to play at any given point in the show, you are thinking about how people can get to and from their instruments or how their instruments can be got to them and how open or fluid the space needs to be to allow that process. (Peter Rowe)

Directing actor-musician shows requires a rebalancing of the hierarchies that govern the making of theatre. The needs of the text may well be the starting point, but of equal consideration are the instruments themselves and the implications they have for almost every element of the process, from design to lighting, from casting to choreography. This shift in emphasis demands a high level of collaboration between the director and the rest of the creative team, to a degree unmatched in other models of theatre making:

> I think what is so liberating about actor-musicianship is that everything is in the melting pot and only when it's all together and it's collaborative and it's messy and it's mashed up does it then become exciting and work. Thinking of musicianship, text work and choreography as separate is never going to be a good experience. (Nikolai Foster)

Directors working in this field need to open their process to include all elements of the production. Movement and music calls may well be led by the choreographer or musical director, but for most directors of actor-musician work there needs to be a fluidity and overlap between disciplines that reflects the interdisciplinary nature of the form.

> There should be no territory. I might, for example, work with a choreographer by suggesting an idea of how the routine might look or I could go to the MD with a basic musical idea which she might then make sense of. It's not about being a control-freak, it is just about being inspired about a project ... The instrument has to come first.
>
> When we did *Animal Farm*, for example, which was my first actor-musician show, I remember thinking that the instruments

were like a whole new group of props. From the outset I didn't want a line of instruments in a separate area and the actors moving over to collect them when they were needed, so we started with the instruments scattered across the floor and from there they went to all manner of places as part of the look of the show. In order to get them for the next scene the actors were forced to make interesting journeys that were born out of the challenge of getting ready to play. I learnt early on that you treat them like a prop or an actor or as part of the choreography. You have to stitch them into the sinew and the fabric of the piece, as you would with any other element of your staging, your choreography or your design. (Nikolai Foster)

This need for fluidity is echoed in the structure of actor-musician rehearsal processes. As an ensemble practice you rarely see calls for individuals or small groups of actors. Scenes have to be rehearsed by the full company, as those involved in music-making are as much a part as those involved directly in the stage action, which presents its own problems and opportunities. The work requires a level of stamina from the actors that has to be respected by those leading rehearsals: the simple fact that actor-musicians have to learn both the text and the music means that there comes a point when you simply cannot progress until this information has been processed, so a weekend break or well-timed recap is as important as driving through. By the same token the constant presence of the music allows for experimentation and play in a way unmatched by traditional musical theatre rehearsal models. As a result many directors have developed quite open approaches to rehearsal:

I still go into rehearsals not knowing what is going to happen and really do hardly any preparation at all. I think about it, I listen to it and make notes. I read it a few times, but I don't do any homework. And now of course I have to say to American actors 'don't do any homework – don't any of you come in here tomorrow having planned what you are going to do with this scene, I can smell it out and it's not allowed in this room'. And this is very difficult, because for them the thought of failing is just too terrifying for words, and actually what I am saying is 'please fail' because your failure might give the answer. That might provide exactly what we need. If I do too much homework or preparation I deny the potential of what is in the room. (John Doyle)

Many of the most powerful moments in actor-musician shows are discovered through play and experimentation or as a result of problem solving. The striking use of the two cellos in John Doyle's *Sweeney Todd*, for example, was the unintentional result of the casting process. Both the actors playing Joanna and Anthony happened to play cello, and Doyle then found ways in which the instruments could echo the connection between the two characters within the story, the result becoming so much a part of the language of the production that all subsequent casts required an Anthony and Joanna who played cello. Similarly the pivotal moment in his critically acclaimed Broadway production of *Company* came from a need to solve a problem:

At one point Bobby goes to the piano and, having not played throughout the show, he starts to play and sing 'Being Alive'. This all came about on a hot Thursday afternoon. I came back from lunch thinking that I had to make something of the fact that he was the only person on the stage who did not play an instrument. I had always wanted to cast a Bobby who could not play – they could all play and he couldn't and that is kind of what the story is. But I came back from lunch thinking, 'what the hell am I going to do?' And I just said to Raul. 'Do you play the piano?' And he said, 'I can sort of play some chords, but I am not really a pianist.' And I said: 'Well I think he should go to the piano and play the beginning of *Being Alive*.' I didn't plan for it to be the linchpin of the production that it turned out to be. I mean grown-ups left sobbing when it happened, it was hugely moving, but it came out of asking what's available.

It is of course common in many rehearsal rooms for directors to make discoveries as part of the process; what is significant in these examples, however, is the fact that these discoveries are about the musical fabric of the show. The presence of the music and musicianship in the space allows for a level of interplay that is not possible when professional musicians are used in traditional musical theatre models. As we have discussed in earlier chapters, the key difference between actor-musicians and musicians is that for them the music is connected to the process of story telling and character in a very direct way, the conditions of their employment, the culture of the actor-musician process and the performer's primary focus as actors, enables the director to access the music in the same way they access any other element of the actor's work. The important thing is finding a way in, the confidence to expand your thinking to include the music and the physical presence of the instruments. Nikolai Foster, as we will explore later, uses early music rehearsals as a chance to begin this process. Here he talks of an example from a music rehearsal for *The Hired Man*:[1]

> We did an early play through of the music and I put them in two lines and said: 'Let's make this an active thing, not just a marking through of what we have learnt.' We got to the First World War, which was a section that I was not sure how to stage, and I am not sure whether they had discussed this or whether it just happened, but they got their chairs and their instruments and they just threw them into the middle of the room and created a barricade and then we were in the trenches – in an instant guitars were becoming machine guns and it was just so moving and powerful. The whole week's music call had built up to this moment of release really and I just looked at it and thought: 'Well this is how we stage it.' We now know how to do the First World War: it is a pile of chairs with the instruments sewn between.

This sort of fluidity requires a flexible approach to the arranging and musical direction, which we will examine later on, but what the example reminds us is that even the process of learning the music is part of the acting journey and as a result there is always a place for the director in these calls.

The process may facilitate a level of discovery and play, but still the pragmatics that govern actor-musicianship must be addressed. For Peter Rowe this requires substantial preplanning and negotiation:

> The success of a good actor-musician treatment of a musical depends on a lot of careful planning in advance. What feels seamless and easy and natural in production has actually taken quite a lot of preplanning and negotiating between the director, the musical director and the choreographer and designer. I think that some people who haven't tackled it before may not be aware of the importance of that level of meticulous planning. It is really vital to get all of that right from the beginning.

As Rowe reminds us the framing of the music and the music-making must be established or discussed in the very earliest stages of pre-production, requiring a level of collaboration between the key creative team that does not suit everyone. It is no surprise that John Doyle, for instance, chose to design some of his own actor-musician work, including *Sweeney Todd*, and was also credited as choreographer as well as directing *Company.* Other directors like Bob Carlton, Glen Walford and Peter Rowe rely on longstanding collaborations with trusted and like-minded designers, choreographers and MDs. Actor-musicianship may not require directors who can do everything, but it certainly calls for individuals who are open to the very particular demands that music makes on a process. The musicianship cannot be approached as an after-thought or add-on. It is central to the language of the piece both in terms of its content and aesthetic and as such it must be considered as part of the dramaturgical framework that underpins the piece.

Selecting material

> I would say that these days you have to make a choice why you are *not* having your actors playing instruments rather than the other way round. (Nikolai Foster)

Although an increasing number of musicals, such as *Once* and *The Commitments*, are being written and created with actor-musicians in mind, the most common use of actor-musicianship is in the reworking of extant musicals. For directors interested in this form of reinvention, what factors should govern the choice of material? What makes a suitable musical for actor-musicians? Peter Rowe offers one perspective:

> What often works are shows that have music in the story. *Guys and Dolls* has a Salvation Army band, *Sugar*[2] has an all-girl orchestra, quite often rock musicals end up being about bands or music-makers or songwriters and if there is music already in the story then that is a really good starting point. You have to think carefully about how the ensemble is going to be present. What relation will they have to the telling of the story? It needs to be a story that requires that sort of ensemble story telling.

John Doyle's career has been very much defined by his actor-musician reinventions of classic musicals, and for him the choice is governed by a range of criteria and sensitivities:

> It is very easy to identify the ones that should not be done with actor-musicians. Like do not do *West Side Story* please, because the art form of that show is an expression through dance and should remain so … It all comes down to why you are using actor-musicians. *Allegro*, which is a musical by Rodgers and Hammerstein that has never really worked, I felt had the opportunity to be told this

way. It is a sort of 'Our Town: the Musical', and it has an opportunity to be told by an America family who are making music together. The company are fundamentally a Greek chorus who are telling this everyman story and so you have a choral element to the piece which allows you to have actor-musicians … You have a responsibility to be respectful. You have to look at what the piece is telling you, which is why I didn't do *Passion* with actor-musicians. It felt inappropriate … Pieces that work for actor-musicians must have music that is indigenous to the culture of the piece or they should already contain a flight of fancy, like *Man of La Mancha* or *Irma La Douce*. I met someone in New York once who said she had seen this strange version of *Irma La Douce* at the Watermill and I said: 'Oh that was ours, what do you remember of it?' And she said she remembered some people lying on a table as if it were a boat and someone playing an accordion like it was the water lapping. And there it was, this image lying in someone's head, because it was a flight of fancy.

For Stephen Sondheim, Doyle's actor-musician reworking of *Sweeney* released the darker elements of the piece, coming closest to his original intention of Grand Guignol.[3] When asked by Doyle if he thought any other of his shows might work well for actor-musicians, he was quick to suggest *A Little Night Music* 'because when I wrote it I thought of each character as an instrument and that is why the boy plays the cello to this day'.[4] Fearing that this was 'a little obvious' he eventually settled on *Company*, telling Doyle 'I just have a feeling that you might be able to bring something out of it that hasn't been seen before'. John Doyle recalls his reaction to the production:

I remember he came and saw it in Cincinnati. When he came out at the end he looked ashen, and I thought 'God he's hated it', and he said: 'I had no idea that we had written a tragedy.' And I said: 'Is that bad?' And he replied: 'Oh no, I just thought it was a musical comedy.' 'But it is about a man who is having a breakdown, who is going through the most terrible night of his life, how could you think that?' And he said: 'You are not a director at all, you are a Cubist.' And I know what that means. The way you have to come at it from another point of view. And he was absolutely right, because to me *Company* was a show where actor-musicianship truly formed the glue that gave the story unity. A unity that probably it had never had before.

Nikolai Foster has directed a number of very successful actor-musician reworkings of musicals, including a version of *Calamity Jane* that premiered at the Watermill Theatre in 2014 before touring the UK. For Foster actor-musicianship is a means of breathing new life into material that could otherwise be dismissed as old-hat.

I think it is just so old-ashioned to put a group of musicians in a pit because music in a musical is as much a part of the narrative as the lyric. A lot of musicals were written originally for a large orchestra, a dancing chorus of 25 and ten principals, but those times are gone. To make something like *Calamity Jane* feel contemporary, for example, and it is very modern in many ways, about the birth of a new country, sexism, sexuality and sexual identity, I as a director can make sure that the music of the story is told visually, as you might do with the props or words or anything else.

Like the current interest in chamber treatments of musicals, actor-musicianship can be seen as a means of subverting the spectacle-driven block-busting model of musical theatre, helping to generate new audiences and interest from those directors who might not otherwise have been drawn to musicals. This is certainly the case for young and emerging director Tom Spencer, whose company Fine Chisel describe themselves as a folk-band and a theatre company. For him actor-musicianship is a route to creating and reinventing work that encourages a new, perhaps younger audience who enjoy its interactivity and immersive nature. Ultimately, however, whatever the criteria that govern the choice of material Peter Rowe suggests that directors need to believe that the actor-musician style is going to 'enhance and give the show a form that is for them better than a conventional production would be'. It is not, perhaps, the default position for the telling of all musical stories, but if directors are to avoid being accused of gimmickry its use has to be thought through. What is sure, however, is that the process offers the director greater access to the music and as a result is a terrifically rewarding experience for those directors who, like Bob Carlton, Doyle and Foster, are deeply musical without being musicians themselves. It certainly seems that once directors discover this form they find it very hard to leave it alone with most, like Rowe, Carlton and Doyle, returning to actor-musicianship time and time again throughout their careers.

Casting

Casting actor-musician shows is a complex business. There are the usual demands of the piece to bear in mind, such as character type, gender and vocal range, but added to that is the need to create a musical ensemble that can achieve the score. If there is to be dance in the production there might also be the need for movement or specific dance skills. David Grindrod, who has cast a number of West End actor-musician productions, recounted the difficulty of responding to the various elements of the casting process for *Once*:

> They have to show their instrumental skill to a really high standard and then you get the next bit where they have to then act, so they come in and work with John Tiffany and then they come in and do the movement bit and Steven Hoggett then says no. And you just have to start looking again.

Directors need to have a sense of how the musicianship is going to work in performance, collaborating with choreographer and MD to find a balance that is reflected in the casting. Pianists and drummers may be difficult to cast as central characters, for example, due to the physical restrictions that their instruments present. Similarly brass and woodwind players cannot sing and play at the same time and so this has implications for both musical arrangements and logistics. Many directors go through the piece prior to casting with the creative team, plotting which characters will need to be free to sing, deciding when and how the music-making will be used in order to facilitate the casting process.

> Even when you have a convention that says they all play, sometimes the focus is so strong that a character that can't know something that happens within the story, might need to be offstage when that moment occurs. When we were doing *Somewhere in England*,[5] for example, it was really critical that an event was a complete shock to a character when it arrived and so we took that actor out of the musical lineup when it happened. You just judge that on a case-by-case basis, there are no hard and fast rules. I remember at the Everyman when the baddie played bass in the panto bands, the children in the audience would boo, so we ended up either taking him out or putting a cover-up cloak on. (Peter Rowe)

There might be a musical conceit that leads the casting process. John Doyle's actor-musician version of *The Wizard of Oz* at the Watermill, for example, used country music for the rural elements of Dorothy's journey and a Dixieland jazz feel when she reached Munchkinland and Oz. We very soon found ourselves looking for a Mayor of Munchkinland who played the sousaphone and a banjo-playing Scarecrow. The requirements can be very specific and not always easy to respond to for agents and casting directors. Nikolai Foster described a more nuanced approach when casting *Calamity Jane*:

> There is a character that the script suggests is an accordion player, but the guy we wanted to go with plays the ukulele and we thought

that it felt right, somehow the ukulele occupies the same sort of territory as the writer meant with the squeezebox. So the instruments do not always lead the process. I am more interested in getting the right feel and then making it work in terms of the music. There are examples where the music might lead. So in *Calamity Jane* Catherine Jayes [the MD] said she needed two violins and we knew that had to be included in the casting process. Also when it came to finding the swings for the show, we had to cast people who could play the right range of instruments and so that is where that journey began. In most cases, however, I think it is always about finding the best person and then making it work musically.

Actor-musicianship is an ensemble art form and so this consideration must also play its part in a director's thinking. John Doyle's casting process is as much about finding the right type of person as the right skillset. He is looking to balance his casts and create a group that can function as an ensemble and be sympathetic to his approach. Like many directors Doyle uses the same performers time and again, sometimes even picking or writing material with them in mind. Bob Carlton formed Rhythm Method with his original *Return to the Forbidden Planet* cast, eventually co-producing the West End version of the show, and maintained a policy of through-casting shows while he was at The Queens Theatre in Hornchurch. For him creating the ensemble is a crucial element of the casting process and one that has a number of advantages:

It's always a mix, and this is one of the strengths of having a through-cast company. There's always some who can act a bit and they are watching someone who has a bit more experience of acting and learning from them and then just the same, the hot rhythm guitarist in breaks is showing the lead guitarist exactly how that riff works and that's the beauty of it, they are all learning from each other.

Who am I when I am playing my trumpet?

> If you are watching an actor-musician using a guitar and the actor is good and he is saying the text and incorporating the guitar there is something in the actor's imagination that invites you to think bigger and better about what you are seeing. (Paddy Cunneen)

Achieving the sort of integration that Paddy Cunneen refers to is largely in the hands of the actor-musician, though directors nonetheless play their part. The framing or stage convention that holds the actor-musicianship is a crucial element for both actor and audience.

> It is really important to establish the convention early on. As an acting company you inherit the convention from the director, but the precise relationship of the chorus to the action can be critical. It plays a massive part in focusing the audience's attention towards the central story. The physical space between the central story and the company watching, the attitude with which they are watching, all of that informs the audience's angle on the story. (Peter Rowe)

There are a number of choices that face actor-musicians when they are playing music. They may be contributing to a scene that their character does not witness or supporting a moment that has a direct bearing on their own storyline. The conceptual framing will sometimes offer an answer, but this is not always the case. One common solution is for the show to have a choral or storytelling dimension to it, suggesting that the company are a group of players engaged in acts of transformation either playing instruments or characters in response to the needs of the story. This choice offers a solution of sorts, but there is still the question of who the company members are when not in character. Directors may need to invest in rehearsal time to explore this extra level of reality or perhaps use music rehearsals to encourage the company to begin to identify as a group in their own right, allowing the relation-ships suggested in the music-making or through the instruments to be the starting point for character and group identity. Actor-musicians may be skilled in their discrete skill sets, but the act of combining acting and music-making is not necessarily something they will find easy.

> Maybe it is because of their training or the fact that they have got so much to get into their heads. I know for example that just singing and playing at the same time is really difficult, but I think that sometimes actor-musicians think very technically. Maybe they haven't worked with a director or choreographer who cares about their instruments. On a very practical level it may be that they are used to thinking about where their instrument is at any given point and are not used to that being dealt with as part of the staging or choreography, which can then make them think in very technical ways and stop them thinking poetically and intuitively. Often my job as a director is to ensure that they are at all times thinking creatively and imaginatively. I say, 'we'll find a way to get you over there, trust me' and the most interesting way to get them over there will be the imaginative way and not the practical way. But in order for us to do that the performer needs to be on the same page as I am, which is thinking creatively, about telling the story and how that character is present in that moment. (Nikolai Foster)

The interplay between instrument and character can be used as a starting point for building character or can be discovered through play. The very sensual physicality of the cello, for example, is often an inspiration for directors and actor-musicians alike; it works well as a signifier of affection or sensuality, offering a way in to the actor's imagination. The guitar solo in so many rock'n'roll shows is another good example of how performance aesthetics from the world of music-making can be used to help actors find a way of uniting their musical expression with a character intention, either reaching out or posturing to audience or other characters in the story.

In *James and the Giant Peach*[6] the cricket's long limbs were described by the bow of the violin. But then it begs the question whether or not these ideas are choices or just connections made by the audience. I am sure, for example, in *Calamity Jane* there will be moments where the audience may think 'oh that moment is a clever directorial or design choice', but in reality it is just that it happened to be the instrument that the actor played. (Nikolai Foster)

Actor-musicians and directors can get hung up on justifying the presence of the instruments or using psychological reasoning rather than reaching for the more poetic and symbolic meanings that can emerge.

I do tend to ban certain questions before we even begin. So I might say: 'I am not going to answer this, this or this about the instruments, because you are going to discover it for yourself.' (John Doyle)

It is largely a matter of confidence and openness on the part of the director, you may not have the solution immediately, but if time is allowed it will become apparent. Rehearsing extant material with actor-musicians is often more akin to devising.

It was really easy with the young people. They would say: 'I can't play my violin in this scene because I am supposed to be in the trenches and they wouldn't have a violin there.' And I would just say. 'I don't care and neither will the audience, you must just play it as if you were in the trenches. Play it like you are trying to save your friend or kill the enemy.' Choreography is the same, nobody dances in real life and yet actors rarely ask the same question about the movement, so why does it become an issue when they play an instrument – it is about the intention and the connection of the thought and the sensoric passage into the instrument. (Nikolai Foster)

The actor-musician's relationship to their instrument is often complex. Very often they have formed deep-rooted relationships with them, with many having played their instruments since childhood, which brings with it all sorts of textures and latent emotional connections that can be exploited in the work.

> It interests me that cast members ask 'who am I when I am playing my trumpet?' because what I get them to do a lot now is to ask why they play that instrument. What is it that drew them to it in the first place? Who told them to go there, and how do they feel about that? Do they like it? It's interesting how many people hate their instruments and all of that informs the way they work with it. (John Doyle)

Like so much of this work there are many ways to encourage and explore integration. What is certain, however, is that it is something that directors must engage with. The music in an actor-musician show is not the territory of the musical director alone and anyone directing this sort of work must find a way of including the instruments in their approach if they are to create rewarding actor-musician shows for both performer and audience:

> I have never been afraid of working with the instruments, but that is because it has happened for me very gradually in terms of scale. There are matters of taste that operate here too. I tend to not be particularly interested in getting an actor to do a line of dialogue and then play a phrase on the clarinet and then do another line of dialogue and so on. I really like the music as part of the process, but sometimes I see work where I think, 'just put the instruments down and play the scene', so I am probably less in favour of speaking dialogue while you are upside down playing the double bass at the same time. It is just a case of experimenting, you shouldn't do it as a director if you are not interested in the music, and there are those who are not, if you are then you will want to

integrate it and use it to its fullest. But it won't suit every director. (Peter Rowe)

Creating the space: Designing actor-musicianship

If you are doing an actor-musician show, you can't be having sets that look like the original Broadway sets. It just doesn't make any sense at all. You have to take the nature of what the form can do. You have to take that and go all the way; like right down to the other end. (John Doyle)

As with so many other elements of actor-musicianship the creation of a suitable space for your production requires an engagement with the form itself.

Every show has its own demands and parameters and so any good designer should be able to work on an actor-musician show. What some designers coming to it for the first time may not know are things like how much space does a drum kit take up? Those are the sort of practical considerations that you can sometimes get stymied by, so it is really important to help brief a designer on those aspects. Where are the instruments going to be located and how are the cast going to get access to and from them? It is quite a good idea to get the designer to model up the instruments, to model up the drum kit, to model up a piano and to look at how that is going to influence their design, because quite often they can say 'oh the band will be there', but actually they aren't aware of what impact that will make on their design and the paraphernalia that sometimes goes with a band such as mics and fold-back speakers and all of that, if it is a rock show. That can be quite a shock to some first-time designers and directors, they have their pristine design and then all this mess gets put on it. (Peter Rowe)

The space is of course dictated by the needs of the piece and the conceptual framing of the production, but the instruments themselves come with their own visual and cultural connotations and meaning. David Hewson, the musical director of actor-musician company Dumbwise, is sensitive to the impact of certain instruments in the space:

> It is interesting how much cultural baggage comes with an instrument when the audience sees it. If they see a piano, for example, the way the piano looks, whether it is modern or whether it is old, the way it actually sounds, it has so much baggage that comes with it and iconography. It carries its history as an instrument with it, before you even get to the way you play it.

In many ways the instruments and the music can become the setting, suggesting time, place and atmosphere, resulting often in a space that is open and simple, what we might call a poetic space. Mark Bailey, a designer who worked with John Doyle on a number of shows, used to say that all he needed to give him was 'a platform on which to play and no more than that', and that was certainly the case for many of their collaborations. *Carmen*, for example, was told on a simple metal circle, suggestive of both the bullring and the military setting, a fact echoed by the dozens of ammunition boxes that were used to create chairs, mountains and whatever structure the story demanded. For Nikolai Foster the work often suggests the aesthetic of 'poor theatre' with very little actually realized in the design itself, left instead to be described through the action or the instruments:

> When we did *Jungle Book*[7] the clarinet became the snake, which is perhaps an obvious example, but the point is that nothing has to be literal anymore. In *Calamity Jane* the setting is an abandoned

theatre, and so the instruments and props and everything are going to be used to tell the story. It is the instruments that become the stagecoach.

Lighting too needs to be responsive to the integration of music-making. Lighting designer Richard G. Jones, a long time collaborator with John Doyle, talks of the deep knowledge he needs of the show when lighting actor-musician work. Like the director he is present for music calls and relies on the music-making as well as its sound to create light that both moves with the music and highlights the moments of music-making that inform the story. Often in Jones' designs the focus is both on the central moment of storytelling and a moment happening in the band simultaneously, that dual relationship between music-making and the main act of storytelling being used to create a lattice of meaning for the audience. Once again the space must allow for these two moments to co-exist and the director must have this in mind as they stage and pre-plan.

Working with music

Don't compartmentalize anything, don't think of the instruments as instruments. I mean the voice is an instrument and you don't think of someone's voice as separate when they start singing. Just think of everything as a unity. (Nikolai Foster)

The culture of specialism that pervades so much of our arts practice and education is a theme that has been explored in a number of chapters in this book. It seems important, however, to continue this discussion in relation to directors. The level of collaboration required by actor-musicianship challenges many theatre makers. It is not always obvious, for example, how a director can operate within a music rehearsal or simply what language they might use when working with music. It is perhaps helpful, therefore, to offer a few examples of how directors use music rehearsals and music in their processes. Here Nikolai Foster offers an insight into his approach:

> I am musical, but I can't read music. I can follow notes on a page as I hear them but that is all. Sarah [Travis] and I work very collaboratively, when she is teaching the music I will be annoyingly over her shoulder giving the cast thoughts, colours, ideas, senses that I am getting as I learn the music with them. It means that when we start to break down the music to learn it, it doesn't just become a technical exercise, but a sort of understanding of what the music means; after all that is where so much of the meaning of a musical is located. In *The Hired Man*, for example, the music that Howard Goodall has written is very English and part of our cultural make-up, it feels visceral and tribal, so when the cast sing together it has a euphoric quality which you can feed into the acting or in the way they are playing an instrument.

Sometimes the observations in the music rehearsal can be very specific. Actor-musicians will often show sides of themselves when playing that are not apparent when they work with text. Nikolai Foster again:

> There was this one boy who had never acted in his life, he had just been learning guitar in his bedroom and had turned up to audition and we gave him a role, because he seemed so interesting. He was really struggling with acting, but during the music rehearsals you saw the process of making music getting to him and he would begin to stand up and really start to play his guitar in a way that spoke to the piece and described character. The guitar comes with so many modern associations and is in many ways the wrong instrument for *The Hired Man* and yet it somehow disappeared and became an extension of him, because of the intention in his music-making.

For many directors it is fear that prevents them from engaging with musical elements, they may think that they are not qualified or that they require a different skill or language to access that area of the work. It is worth remembering John Blacking's ideas about the very particular way that our culture has chosen to limit the term musician to describe only those who make music, rather than widening the notion to include the listening and appreciation of music that we are all capable of. Simply giving space for music to operate on the imagination is an important element of allowing it to shape and guide a piece. I remember well an evening rehearsal for *Carmen* at the Watermill, when John Doyle simply allowed us to play through the music. There was very little instruction, just gentle encouragement to choose to whom and how we wanted to play. The room was bathed with evening summer sunshine and we just sat or lay about the space simply letting the music act on us and the space. For both director and actors the rehearsal was significant, allowing us all to find out what the music wanted to say, how it might lead us towards the story. The very fact that it was led by the director and not the MD meant that the emphasis shifted away from technical concerns and towards the more open territory of how it sounded and felt in our fingers and to our ears. It was in that sense very much an acting rehearsal.

Nikolai Foster again:

> I'm there at the music calls listening, responding, asking questions, answering questions. Obviously the MD is leading, but I am very much there alive, awake and switched on, because if you set up from the very beginning that they are doing that bit and you are on the phone or doing other stuff, then how on earth is this ever going to be a collaborative exercise ... What I am most alive to weirdly is when someone is trying to learn something and they are not connecting to it or are finding it difficult. I intuitively know that is a very good time to drop in an idea or something that is not connected to the technical aspect of what they are doing, but is more about the poetry or the imaginative response, in order to make something relax

or to trigger something that will enable them to find it. Sometimes you can gain understanding from the technical perspective and the director can build ideas on top of that, but at other times the psychological idea will unlock things technically or musically. Sarah [Travis] will often say: 'I don't care if some of these notes are wrong as long as you are committing to it and making a sound that is telling the story.' That approach is far more harmonious on all levels than playing it without feeling or a sense of connection to the narrative.

Peter Rowe uses the music calls as a time to develop directorial ideas:

Most of the time I am sitting absorbing the music and thinking about how it is going to influence the staging: where the musical turning points are, what the tempo of the song is like and how we are going to achieve that on stage. I am just soaking all that up. The practicalities of who is playing what and when and how that is going to impact on who is going to do what where. You have to get the music inside your bones, because the success of the production is really about the rhythm of the whole event and the music is a big part of that. You want everything to be working to the same changes of tone and tempo.

Directors may be nervous of music, but actor-musicianship is dependent on the music being absorbed into the process of rehearsal and not siloed into music calls:

I knew from the get go that I had to get my hands dirty. I couldn't be frightened, I had to attack the actor-musicianship with as much conviction as I would words or singing, so that the instrument didn't become something I was nervous or afraid of. I made a very clear decision right at the beginning. (Nikolai Foster)

Often the skills required in the shaping and use of music are directorial skills. The use of underscore is a good example of music that has a dramaturgical emphasis. A director does not need to compose or create it, but can certainly play a part in how and when it is used:

> The original *Planet* underscore was actually me, who can't write a note of music, going 'it's that bit of 'She's Not There', because it's creepy' and then Kate Edgar would adapt the idea. (Bob Carlton)

Actor-musician shows in fact enable this sort of dialogue and engagement from a director like no other theatre making process:

> What we underscore, how we lead in and out of songs, the nature of the underscoring, where do we have reminders of things that have come in before, are all territory for the director and the brilliant thing about actor-musician shows is that you can decide that in the room, you are not having to go away and consult a composer. You can try that out in the space and that is the most exciting bit. (Peter Rowe)

Directors can and should work with music, it is a crucial part of actor-musicianship, but as Nikolai Foster suggests it may also be a growing emphasis in all theatre making:

> It's amazing to think that the music might be able to express the anger or even sexual frustration of a character through the way the instrument is played or that you can use the instruments to create a stagecoach or the First World War. I think we are on the cusp of a change: producers used to think it was cheap to create an actor-musician show, but we are in some sort of middle period now when we are more accepting of the use of music in theatre and I think that in a few years' time there will be no need to label it, we will just see a lot more integration of instruments and other forms of musical expression in shows.

An act of reinvention

> I was very proud to get a letter from Hal Prince when the show was
> in London, saying: 'I just want to thank you. Thank God at last I
> have gone to see a *Sweeney Todd* that wasn't a copy of my own
> production.' (John Doyle)

Hal Prince's letter to John Doyle is an interesting reminder of the
dilemma that faces directors of actor-musician versions of extant
musicals. On the one hand the process offers a means of reinvention,
a way for them to make their mark and yet on the other there is
the issue of performance rights and intellectual property. Actor-
musicianship may be difficult to define as a genre in its own right, but
if the problems encountered by some directors are anything to go by,
it is certainly viewed as a radical departure from the norm by many
lawyers and publishers. Actor-musicianship may open up musicals to
new audiences, but it does in turn pose a problem for those directors
wishing to work with extant material.

> It is different now because I am known for that, but when I think
> back to *Fiddler* at the Watermill it was a very different story. The
> lawyers came after the good reviews appeared in the national
> papers, and said: 'We will let this finish its run here, but it is going
> nowhere else, and the Americans must never know that this
> happened.' Several years later I was in Patti LaPone's dressing
> room in the last week of previews of *Sweeney Todd*, and there
> was an elderly man there and Patti said: 'John I'd like you to meet
> Joe Stein.' The name didn't really mean anything to me at first and
> I got talking to this man, and as I was talking to him I realized it
> was Joseph Stein, who wrote the book for *Fiddler*. He said to me:
> 'Have you ever thought of doing *Fiddler on the Roof* this way?' And
> I said: 'I have already.' He said: 'Could you come to my apartment
> for breakfast tomorrow morning?' So I went to his apartment on

Park Avenue the next morning and I told him what we'd done with it. How all these people had gathered round a Sabbath table with their instruments and how the story was told from within that framing, and he started to cry and he said: 'How can we not know about this?' I said: 'You didn't know because what I did was illegal, and a breach of the rights agreement.' I think it is an artist's job is to challenge legality, if you feel a story has got to be told, you should tell that story, with the means that are available to you as long as you are being truthful to that story. And I felt our version was really very truthful to the story. And it is just so bizarre to have the writer later saying: 'could you do it like that?'

Doyle's experience is a reminder of just how grey this area can be. In the case of work by living writers or composers it may well be possible to engage them in the process of adaptation: that was certainly the case for his 1999 production of *Irma La Douce*, which saw writers Julian More and Monty Norman collaborating with Doyle and MD Catherine Jayes. Despite initial fears about cuts, Stephen Sondheim has also become a keen supporter of actor-musicianship. He was instrumental in Doyle's *Sweeney Todd* coming to Broadway and, as has already been discussed, was complicit in the later adaptation of *Company*. Andrew Lloyd Webber was at first resistant to actor-musician versions of his work, until Craig Revel Horwood's reworking of *Sunset Boulevard* at the Watermill in 2008. This was in part due to Horwood's own professional record, having been involved in mainstream musical theatre for a number of years, including as Associate Choreographer of the original West End production of *Martin Guerre,* which had enabled him to get permission to do an actor-musician reworking of *Guerre* in 2007 paving the way for the 2008 version of *Sunset.* Without these sorts of relationships, however, it is the impact on the music that makes actor-musician interpretations of extant work a somewhat tricky affair for directors wishing to navigate the complex area of performing rights.

It is all part of the reinvention of the work. The music in *Calamity* was originally conceived as a big orchestral thing, but we wanted it to sound more like bluegrass, that people from a frontier town might play. I mean most of these blokes would not have been interested in playing music, they were too busy killing Indians and raping the land for its gold, but if they were to sensitively sit down and start leching over pictures of naked women, then what instrument might they pick up? Well it would probably be a shabby old guitar or honky-tonk piano and they'd make bluegrass music. So in the flick of a switch almost, we are able to reinvent that whole piece, as the musical landscape changes in response to the use of instruments as part of the action. (Nikolai Foster)

This change of musical emphasis certainly needs to be negotiated with most publishers, but with the current high profile and relative longstanding of actor-musicianship, it is not an insurmountable problem. Nikolai Foster had to provide a rationale for the changes he proposed to *Calamity Jane* before getting the go-ahead. Peter Rowe's 2014 actor-musician production of *The Threepenny Opera* required permission from the notoriously strict Kurt Weill estate. The show was a co-production with disabled theatre company GRAEAE and so the needs of the performers as well as the actor-musician elements made for some tricky negotiation:

They were very strict, but it was also absolutely straightforward in that they said 'you can do the show as long as you do the arrangements absolutely as written and in the original keys'. We took a little bit of license in that people were playing the original score, but sometimes on different devices, but every note was there. We haven't had a lot of trouble with that, you have to ask permission and there is sometimes negotiation and you do need someone to battle for you. It has taken a long time sometimes, but we have never actually been refused.

Finding a sympathetic producer is certainly part of the battle. It is unlikely, for instance, that John Doyle's successes at The Watermill would have been possible without the tenacity and risk taking of the then Artistic Director, the late Jill Fraser. Similarly it was Edward Stern's vision that saw *Company* being reinvented by actor-musicians at Cincinnati Playhouse:

> You need a producer who will support you. But as an artist, it is really hard, you can't listen to the voices in your own head or in anybody else's head for that matter. You just have to do what you need to do. And if that gets you into trouble well … nobody is going to die. It's not that kind of trouble. (John Doyle)

A more complicated notion of ownership, however, can be found in the very nature of the actor-musician process itself:

> Actor-musicians, and particularly those who have worked together a lot, have a tremendous sense of ownership over the work, in a way that is not the case with normal actors, because they are an aural soundscape as well as everything else and that demands a tremendous amount of emotional commitment and therefore personal commitment. Now there is no answer to this, except to say that if you ask a group of adults to come into a room and be playful like this, how do you maintain the boundaries? It is very complicated to give ownership in a rehearsal room, and yet at the same time to reserve what is and what is not one's own work. (John Doyle)

When the work is written or created by the director such as in the case of Bob Carlton's *Return to the Forbidden Planet* the notion of ownership may be slightly easier to define, although the 1989 London production was co-produced by members of the cast, the actual rights to the show belonged to Carlton as writer. As with so much in actor-musician practice, however, the director has to be aware that the integration of the instruments is not simply a convenient way of reducing cost. It is an artistic choice that can amount to a wholesale reinvention of extant musicals. The best and most rewarding actor-musician experiences are always going to be those that are embarked on with the integration of music as the starting point. It may not suit all directors, but for those who do work in this way the rewards of actor-musicianship are many and the possibility it offers for directors to engage in every aspect of the language of the show clearly irresistible to those who, like the contributors to this chapter, have returned frequently to the imaginative release this theatre form enables.

Notes

1   Nikolai Foster directed and Sarah Travis MDed an actor-musician version of Howard Goodall and Melvyn Bragg's musical adaptation of Bragg's novel *The Hired Man* for the National Youth Music Theatre. The production premiered in London's St James Theatre, August 2014.

2   Frank Loesser, Jo Swerling and Abe Burrows' musical *Guys and Dolls* was given an actor-musician reworking by Peter Rowe, with musical arrangements and direction by Greg Palmer in 2011. The production premiered at The New Wolsey Theatre in Ipswich before touring. Peter Stone, Jule Styne and Bob Merrill's musical *Sugar*, a reworking of *Some Like It Hot,* was given an actor-musician treatment by the same team in 2005, premiering again in Ipswich.

3   Stephen Sondheim interviewed by Charles Isherwood for *New York Times*, 'Cutting *Sweeney Todd* to the Bone', 30 October 2005.

4   Sondheim quoted by John Doyle in an interview done for this publication.

5   *Somewhere in England* a new play by Mike James, premiered at Theatr Clwyd, October 2014.

6   David Wood's stage adaptation of *James and the Giant Peach* was given an actor-musician retelling by Nikolai Foster for Birmingham Stage Company in 2012. The production started at The Old Rep in Birmingham before touring the UK.

7 Stuart Patterson's version of *The Jungle Book* played at Glasgow Citizen's Theatre over Christmas 2013. The show was directed and MDed by Nikolai Foster and Sarah Travis, with music and lyrics by B. B. Cooper and Barb Jungr.

5

CHOREOGRAPHING ACTOR-MUSICIANSHIP

The use of movement and dance in actor-musician work varies in scale and scope enormously, depending on the nature of the piece and the tastes of the creative team. In many cases the act of playing instruments is offered as the main choreographic element, as the activity is compelling and physically busy thereby reducing the need for additional or extraneous movement or dance. John Doyle, for instance, has often created actor-musician work without using a choreographer, developing the physical language of the piece as an extension of his role as director. In much of his early work in York and at the Watermill he would work with a dance captain from within the company, using a basic movement vocabulary to create musical staging that emerged from the rehearsal process. This was also the case in some of his more recent productions including the Cincinnati and Broadway versions of *Company*, prompting this response from one reviewer:

> Though Doyle is credited as director-choreographer, there's little actual choreography here, and it is missed in a few places.[1]

When it comes to applying actor-musicianship to pieces from the musical theatre canon, there is often an expectation from audiences, as well as a requirement from the piece itself for dance. Shows such as *Cabaret* are hard to achieve without a choreographic element, similarly Peter Rowe's recent actor-musician version of *Guys and Dolls* and Nikolai Foster's *Calamity Jane* have dance sewn into the fabric of the storytelling. Craig Revel Horwood's actor-musician shows have dance as their starting point, due to the fact that Horwood is himself a choreographer and director. His effusive style embraces the inclusion of the instruments in the same way that it has in the past embraced scenographic and visual elements in non-actor-musician work: I recall his 2001 version of Shostakovich's *Paradise Moscow* at London's Sadlers Wells directed by David Pountney, which saw larger-than-life kitchen utensils used as part of a hugely theatrical vision for the choreography. For Horwood the move to include instruments seems a natural extension of his style and approach; for many choreographers, however, the particular challenge of integrating instruments and working with actor-musicians is something that requires consideration. This chapter is an attempt to respond to this need, by examining the contrasting approaches of two choreographers who have worked in this area. Francesca Jaynes, who is perhaps best known for her work in film, such as Tim Burton's *Sweeney Todd, Alice in Wonderland* and *Charlie and the Chocolate Factory* and the Oscar winning *Gravity*, has been working with actor-musicians since the 1980s, first at Liverpool Everyman and then at a number of theatres including the Bubble and Ipswich's New Wolsey. Steven Hoggett, Olivier Award winner and Tony-nominated choreographer and founder of Frantic Assembly, has an equally eclectic body of work including the West End and Broadway productions of *The Curious Incident of the Dog in the Nighttime.* In this chapter he talks about his approach to the choreography for the Tony Award-winning *Once*, a show created for a cast of actor-musicians that has enjoyed international acclaim.

Steven Hoggett

Most choreography processes begin with music, and for Steven Hoggett this extends to the score itself; the rise and fall of the notation on the page offering a suggestion of physical form. In the case of *Once* the actor-musicianship offered Hoggett the opportunity to expand this exploration of musical shape into the physicality of music-making, as he outlines in this description of the inspiration for the choreography for *Gold*, the show's most fully realized moment of dance:

In the first couple of hours of every day Martin [Lowe, the MD] would teach the performers the music. They were all just sat in chairs and basically I would watch them learn. At times they were ergonomically wrapping themselves around their instruments, trying to look at a fret board or when somebody else was playing you would see them fall off to the side of their seats or see their bodies move as they listened. I was sitting behind them or to the side, which meant I was watching their spines a lot of the time and I could see where their weight was falling in their heads and in their shoulders. Just what the human body does when it hears a beautiful phrase played … I took a note of all these bodily shapes that were happening while they were listening to themselves learn the music for the show, and *Gold* really is just about those moves. All those positions, dynamics and movements are based on what they did rehearsing the music … In some ways they were unaware what I was doing and I didn't even know that it would give me enough to create a three and a half minute piece. But once I started noting the details of what they were doing, there was a lot to work with.

The very process of music-making and the particular way in which that original workshop company applied themselves to the task gave Hoggett an entire choreographic vocabulary, allowing the movement to emerge from the rehearsal process. As with the performer's integration of instruments, the physical language of *Once* became an extension of the music, creating the sense of a musical space within which the show exists. The process was not always synergous, however, certain moves had to be altered or borrowed for application at different points of the show:

In a way the choreography emerged from the playing, but often the moves were done by people who were listening. I can remember when Elizabeth, the original violinist, first played the repeated falling phrase and Lucas put his head back in this gorgeous movement as if to say 'Oh that's beautiful'. In terms of the cadence of that line I knew that Lucas putting his head back wouldn't make sense of the falling phrase; so Lucas's move went in, but it went somewhere else. I liked the move itself, but it didn't concord with the musical phrase.

Hoggett's journey as choreographer mirrors the experience of directors outlined in earlier chapters: as so often happens in actor-musician rehearsals, it was the process of music-making that became the crucible for the creative process; a moment shared with Martin Lowe, the show's musical director and arranger. The original conceit for the choreography of *Once* had been an exploration of 'being in love in Dublin', but finding this too limiting, Hoggett was left without a starting point when the workshop process began.

A lot of it came from throwing out the original idea for the choreography and having nothing else in its place. *Once* wasn't meant to be going anywhere, it wasn't lined up to go to Broadway, it wasn't meant to be in the West End, it was just a try-out and the producers were very generous in the way that they made you constantly feel like that. I was in the position of starting the process without an idea, so it was fascinating to rely on a group of people that did not realize that they were providing the choreography by sitting for two hours every morning trying to learn music. What the actor-musicianship offered me as choreographer was access to the layering of the music – just the fact that Martin [Lowe] was changing things as he was teaching it. I got a sense of where the groundswell of the music was happening. I got a sense of when they became a full community and when they became slightly more isolated.

In many cases the conditions that govern the making of theatre require choreographers to work independently, to prepare in advance to recordings or to work with musicians who are not integrated in the rehearsal process. Actor-musicianship by contrast, offers an opportunity for choreographers to work in synergy with the learning of the musical elements. This enabled Hoggett to develop a deep knowledge of the music of *Once* that extended to the physical act of music-making itself and it was this, coupled with the freedom allowed by the producers, that was fundamental to his choreographic process, eventually offering ideas that related not only to the performers, but the instruments themselves:

> In the second act there is a kind of breakdown, where all the instruments are in tornado effect, the idea being that this is a point when the characters are in a kind of vortex not knowing quite where to put themselves. We were able to make a one minute 20 second piece of music that Martin [Lowe] wrote for the show, where the instruments were aping the emotional state of the performers. It was almost like a reversal of process, asking what the instruments would do if they were confused and frustrated and didn't know what was going on. Towards the end of rehearsals it seemed right to be working with the instruments and making them spin or explode and lose a sense of themselves. It was almost as if they were now doing the kind of thing that the actors would usually be doing.

For Hoggett choreographing *Once* was not about making musicians dance, but more an act of 'unwrapping' the inner musicality inherent in the act of playing and listening to music. This change of emphasis is hard to articulate, but it became apparent when the show eventually came to London:

> It was only when we taught the show to the London cast that I realized that having musicians dancing is not what we intended for

Once and it doesn't look right when people are kind of kicking it out. There is something about the internal nature of the show that reflects something about musicianship. The learning of a piece of music is a very internal, introspective, personal, private thing that becomes beautifully public, but that process is really essential. It has to be about someone listening to themselves in relation to an instrument and making a privacy public, that is the tricky balance … a quadruple-threat is just not the right way to think about it, I don't even know what that means. With the choreography of *Once* we were just unwrapping what was inherently happening within a musicians body. I don't think it's suddenly giving them the capacity to do a high kick and a step ball change, it is just making public what most musicians do to some degree. It is just dialling that up or giving that element a bit more focus, but they are not suddenly dancers as well. It is just allowing an element to be more visible.

This act of revealing the inner and introspective world of musicality is reminiscent of the ideas explored in earlier chapters. This almost archaeological endeavour underpins many of the sensitivity training exercises, and can be found in the work of Gardzienice and *Song of a Goat*. It can be found in dance and movement contexts in the work of Rudolf Laban, Dalcroze and Isadora Duncan. Like Steven Mithen's notion of 'Hmmmmm'[2] the innate relationship between music and movement is something that Hoggett uses as his starting point. The result is a mesmerizing performance aesthetic that offers a sense of fluidity between music, character and space. This is not, however, the traditional choreographic fare of musical theatre, a fact reflected in Ben Brantley's *New York Times* review of the show:

This is not music that lends itself to the usual chorus-line kicks and shimmies. Instead, Steven Hoggett … sets the songs to stylized physical movements that are as distinctive and evocative as any Broadway choreography since Bill T. Jones' work on *Spring Awakening*.

Sometimes Mr. Hoggett sends his performers into spirited hoedowns, featuring amiably dueling violinists and dancing on tables. More often they move with calculated tentativeness, in reaching gestures that summon infinite, thwarted longing.

For Brantley it is not so much the actor-musicianship, as the style of music that promotes this 'distinctive' choreographic response from Hoggett. This is certainly an important factor to bear in mind, for as we find in John Doyle's work, even extant musical theatre has to be reworked in actor-musician retellings, resulting in a more intimate, chamber-like feel and sound. This can result in the need for choreography being reduced, as with some of Doyle's work, but as Brantley's suggests, it is also a prompt for new choreographic forms. For Hoggett the solution was to use the instruments and the act of playing as the governing factor, a process that revealed its own set of choreographic rules:

I realized that if they didn't have instruments in their hands then the movement had to be reduced. There was an acapella section that I originally put quite a few movements in, which was a real lesson in how this worked. In the end I took most of the movement out. A few people lean and then a few people look up into the sunlight and that is it … the instruments became the choreographic arc. When the two leads are in the studio and during *Falling Slowly* I only choreographed where they stood and that was it. In those two moments they are singing in a way that is absolutely pure and I didn't feel that choreographically I could add anything.

Even the pragmatics of the music-making played their part in the process, as is so often the case, the actor-musicianship called for a high level of collaboration between choreographer and musical arranger. Martin Lowe's music was often dependent on groups of instruments being close to one another, a factor Hoggett embraced and used to govern some staging choices. In such an intimate ensemble show the choreography even became part of the sound design:

> Even before Clive Goodwin, the sound designer, was involved, I was mindful that we didn't want an amplified show, we wanted it as acoustic in feel as possible, so part of my job was to create a balanced sound. If you have a 27-piece orchestra, you have got so much power that you can have all your strings in one place and your woodwind over there, but when you only have two violins, a cello and three guitars you actually have to be a bit smarter about how that sound comes forward ... I noticed that it just didn't sound very pretty if everything was loaded to stage right ... Martin [Lowe] was generous about it, but I could tell that we just weren't getting the right kind of sound balance on stage and I thought: 'Great, let's make something more interesting and that sounds better.' Nothing about that felt frustrating, it was just a chance to explore, where someone might sit or perch so we can achieve a really nice stage picture, but where the harmonics are working much better.

Despite the synergy between the music and dance, however, the actor-musicians having to achieve Hoggett's choreography still struggled to put all the elements together in rehearsal:

> The longest part of the *Once* process was teaching *Gold* and them trying to play their instrumentation while achieving the choreography. That was a day-by-day thing. You really just had to hold your nerve. I blagged it at the beginning by saying: 'This is absolutely possible,' but I didn't know that for sure ... There's a repeated falling phrase, for example, that I loved and I choreographed a kind of falling motion for each of those. Now that doesn't mean that playing that line became any easier for the performer because of that ... I would always ask them to do the hardest option first of all, but would also ask what was easier for them in terms of playing. So on the first phrase when they are naturally falling away from

their instruments I asked them if it was possible not to look at the fretboard and they said: 'Well right now I am not able to do it, but I should be able to do it in about a week.'

Like any element of actor-musicianship, choreography has to be learned and absorbed by the performer before it can be fully integrated. In most actor-musician processes it is the music that comes first, but the point at which movement is explored is something that the choreographer has to gauge. As a general rule of thumb, and in common with all those who contributed to this book, it is important to get the music on its feet sooner rather than later, but a day-by-day drip-feed approach is often the only way to progress. Some movement is easier to achieve and more harmonious with the act of playing and indeed some instruments lend themselves to movement more than others, as Hoggett reflects:

'The North Strand' is a song that happens at the end of *Falling Slowly* where they are charging across the space in a kind of men versus women … it is kinetic and it moves and travels, which is another challenge all together, but weirdly that was easier for them to achieve. In some ways you can slightly busk the physicality and also I based it on the rhythmic phrases so it follows the playing of chords on the guitar. I used the musical emphasis, whereas *Gold* cuts across the music and is quite tricky.

The emphasis on music-making coupled with the ensemble nature of actor-musicianship meant that Hoggett's work had to extend to the whole stage picture: every movement, even the placing of a chair became part of the musicality of the show; every prop, like the instruments themselves, became part of the show's musical expression. This synergy between music-making and movement offers us an example of how actor-musicianship can lead the process of choreography. Hoggett still faced the issue of how to facilitate and teach his ideas to actors who have so much to manage in performance, but

what we see in *Once* is a methodology and choreographic approach
that is shaped completely by the presence of actor-musicians.

Francesca Jaynes

Francesca Jaynes shares some of Hoggett's responsiveness to
musical imperatives, but for her it is the experience of working
with actors that has offered her a way into actor-musicianship as a
choreographer.

> I just try to work with the actor and the great thing about most
> actors is that they want to make something work and they want
> to be challenged … It's not just about the steps. With dancers you
> tend to tell them what to do and they pick it up so quickly and they
> don't question it, where as actors will and always should question
> why they or their character is doing that move. Crucially with actors
> it is their characters who are dancing, where as with a dancer the
> dancing is their skill and focus. They may well have a character, but
> I am not sure that they focus on that in the way that actors might.
> You always get another layer when you work with actors.

With the exception of *Charlie and the Chocolate Factory*, where
Jaynes' choreography saw Deep Roy experimenting with actor-
musicianship as every member of an Oompa-Loompa rock-band,
her experiences in film have been largely with actors working without
instruments. 'I love working with actors', she says, 'I understand
people who can't dance. I understand their fear.' It is this openness to
the needs of the non-dancer that seems to have informed her ability
to work with actor-musicians, allowing her to adapt her process to
the particular demands of a given instrument or the musical needs
of the piece, in the same way that she adapts to the varying levels of
technical skill and physicality presented by actors.

If they trust you and you trust them, you can just gauge between you if something is going to be impossible with the instrument. I will listen to them and the MD and if they say 'at that point I really don't think that's going to work in terms of the music', then you just find something easier to facilitate the playing. I have never really had to change anything that much … if I do it will often be quite subtle things. I might want them to go on the count of three and they might ask to go half a beat afterwards because that is just easier for what they are playing. You just have to listen and respond to them.

As with Steven Hoggett the instruments also offer inspiration and come with their own rules and sense of character:

The brass are so showy, the instruments themselves are so sparkly that it suggests a style and sense of movement. The shape of the actor-musician's body changes when they play. I try to keep an open mind because as actors they want to be challenged, but there must be a sense that the instruments affect the way you work with them … Brass is always easier to work with partially because they are freer physically. I don't know anything about music and I have never played an instrument, but I know that it seems to be easier for brass players to understand what is in a dancer's head, whereas with guitarists it is often much harder. Physical accents seem to be easier for the brass players to get, to step and then stab, for example, because they are perhaps more used to it as a musical idea.

While a sensitivity to the instruments informs her approach to teaching and working with actor-musicians in the rehearsal room, the process of creating the choreography is informed solely by the music and narrative framing:

I didn't know anything about actor-musicianship when I first started, and so it never occurred to me to choreograph anything other than what I had in my head. The actor-musicians would tell me when they can't do something, so I just went ahead as normal. It has never felt like a compromise to me and that is how I've worked ever since. I try to work purely from the music. I don't imagine the instruments when I am listening to the music in preparation ... When we did *Guys and Dolls*, for example, I wanted to do what the music and the piece suggested to me even though the cast were playing instruments, I didn't want that to influence me at all.

This is a very different starting point from that of Steven Hoggett in *Once* and one that is perhaps more akin to approaches taken by choreographers working in mainstream musical theatre. The defining factor, however, is that her process is mediated by the needs of the performer, whether that be an actor finding dance intimidating or an actor-musician struggling to play and move at the same time. Nonetheless and in common with Hoggett, it is the music that leads the process of teaching the choreography:

I am convinced that the music is the most important element for the actor-musician, if they know the music really well then they can put the steps on top. It is about gauging the individual because some like to work with everything at the same time. You very quickly gauge which people need most attention, whether that is about their instrument, their personality or their ability, you have to work that one out as well.

As in *Once* the ensemble nature of actor-musicianship often means that the choreographer's focus must extend to those supporting the main stage action musically, in a way that would not be replicated if working with musicians:

It is OK for the instruments to be in the background and still be part of the story, they don't have to be in the foreground or central visually all the time … You want to feel that the emotion of the band is the same as the emotion on the foreground stage, that everybody is in the same emotional place. It often happens late in the process, when you have got into the theatre and you are able to sit back. You might realize that someone has to be completely still in that moment or that it would be great if there was a little turn or movement, just to make sure people are present, that can be something really simple like just bringing the energy of the body forward. You have to try to engage everybody, even those playing more challenging instruments in terms of movement. You might just get the drummer to lift an arm at a point when everyone else is doing that in the choreography, if he can. It might be that in the stiller moments you just have to make sure that an eye-line is with everyone else, but again that can be complicated because sometimes eye-lines are dictated by where the musicians have to look to facilitate the music. Sometimes it can just be about reminding them that they are in the same space as the characters directly engaged in the narrative and actors take that on board, they get that.

The ambition for Jaynes is that the use of the instruments becomes a 'seamless' element of the choreography and broader stage aesthetic, which means there may well be moments where the playing is enough:

I have seen shows where instruments are placed in the middle of a danced moment without any clear need in the song's narrative, as if they had been put in just because it was an actor-musician show and so you had to put the instruments in whenever you can. It is not always appropriate. The story has always got to be the most important thing.

Lovely souls

It has not been the ambition of this chapter to define a set of rules or governing principles for working with actor-musicians, but rather to encourage a discussion about the very particular nature of this type of choreographic task through an examination of the work of two people with experience in the field. In the case of Steven Hoggett we find a process that has been shaped completely by the presence of actor-musicians, in Francesca Jaynes we see an approach that is malleable enough to adapt to their varying needs. Whether manifest in the symbiotic relationship between the members of the creative team or the dialogue between choreographer and performer, actor-musicianship requires a level of fluidity between disciplines that is rarely matched in other processes. What unites Hoggett and Jaynes is their willingness to embrace the collaborative nature of actor-musician work. Both share a relish in the process of discovering how their work can be augmented by the presence of the instruments and in the deep collaboration and skill sharing that has to happen between the creative team. Actor-musicianship promotes a culture in the rehearsal room that has been remarked on by all those who have contributed to this book, whether they be performers, directors, MDs or choreographers. There is a sense of shared endeavour and ownership, a culture of openness and generosity that characterizes actor-musicianship; a quality not found to the same degree in other areas of theatre making. It may not suit all theatre makers, but it seems that for those who enjoy it this form of theatre is seductive and something they return to again and again. Perhaps we can end this chapter with a last word on the subject from Francesca Jaynes:

> I worked with puppeteers this year on *Gravity* and *Muppets Most Wanted* and I thought how much they are like actor-musicians because of the level of collaboration. To make Kermit dance you have to have six people all doing tiny little things to make it work,

they are in the background, they hand their talents and their precision over to this inanimate object which they make live and it reminded me of working with actor-musicians, they are just lovely souls.

Notes

1   Michael Portantiere's review of *Company* at Cincinnati Playhouse, for *Theater Mania*, 20 March 2006: http://www.theatermania.com/ohio-theater/reviews/03-2006/company_7871.html (accessed 26 November 2014).

2   Mithen, S., *The Singing Neanderthals* (Cambridge, MA: Harvard University Press, 2008).

6

MUSICALLY DIRECTING ACTOR-MUSICIANSHIP

If you are too bound or tied into the notes then you are not thinking of the other stuff and that is my job, to pull out as much from that moment as possible.

SARAH TRAVIS

Of all the practitioners interviewed for this book, it is the musical directors who have offered the strongest sense of what is distinctive about actor-musicianship as a performance practice, revealing some of the clearest evidence of how the integration of music-making has led to the development of new and particular approaches to theatre making. Both in the UK and the US there have emerged musical directors who have become expert in this area and it is through their work that I would like to examine some of the processes and methodologies best suited for application with actor-musicians. As with other chapters it should not be read as a 'how to' guide, but rather as a means of provoking thought and reflection on how to honour and develop the musical element of actor-musicianship. With the weight of history and accepted practice that exists in mainstream musical theatre it is impossible not to see this chapter, in part at least, as a comparative study; an examination of how the typical role of musical director is affected by the presence of actor-musicians. It is perhaps useful, therefore, to begin with a brief summary of how this role might normally be fulfilled. The function and approach of the musical director is of course dictated in part by the nature of the production and so for the purposes of this chapter we will limit our exploration to what we might broadly define as Musical Theatre, that is work that includes music and song as an integrated part of its dramaturgical structure and performance aesthetic. As in other chapters it is hoped that by reflecting on the most demanding area of actor-musician work, broader conclusions will emerge that can be applied to other contexts and applications.

Mainstream musical theatre practice often requires the presence of a number of roles to support the musical elements of the production. There is firstly the composer and lyricist, who may or may not be the same person, then the orchestrator or arranger, the musical director and in many cases a musical supervisor. The musical director or MD is primarily responsible for liaising between the cast and the musicians. He or she will teach the cast the songs, be present for the majority of their rehearsal process and liaise with the director and choreographer in the shaping and interpretation of the music. In most cases they will then disappear for a day or two in the final stages of rehearsal to work with the orchestra or band. Their job then changes in focus as the musical accompaniment is rehearsed without the presence of actors or singers. This is often a very quick process, lasting only a day or two, using highly skilled musicians who sight-read the score prepared by the orchestrator and realize the music without direct reference to the stage action. In this process the MD acts as a conduit between the musicians and the cast, communicating the nuances that have emerged during the rehearsal process. Finally the MD returns to the rehearsal space with his musicians in tow for the *sitzprobe*, which sees music and cast reunited for what is often a glorious moment of togetherness, before the band retreats to a pit or offstage area as the show moves into the theatre, the MD remaining the only visible evidence of the music for cast and often audience alike. Compare this then to the typical actor-musician show: the MD is present throughout rehearsals; the music is created alongside the stage action; there is no separate band and therefore no last minute band call or *sitzprobe*; with no need for a conduit between musicians and cast, the MD's role diminishes as the show moves into the theatre, their job effectively ending once the show opens. There is often a requirement to return to give notes during the run, but for the MD of an actor-musician show there is usually no conducting role and indeed no dual focus as they work with only one group of performers, who fulfil the role of actor, singer and musician. This shift in process results in a rebalancing of the function and approach from MDs. Actor-musicianship relies more heavily on the teaching element of the job than in the mainstream model. Actor-musicians may often be musically accomplished, but as a band they require a level of facilitation that is not replicated in the professional band call; their primary role as actors creates a very different rehearsal culture when it comes to music-making and a need for nurture that is not as evident in mainstream musical theatre models. Most actor-musician companies contain a wide range of musical approaches and skill levels that must be accommodated. There may well be a need for separate music calls, but in actor-musicianship the music is never the sole focus in performance, with music-making tempered by staging, character work and choreography. Not surprisingly the form does not suit all MDs. It can be seen as a compromise for some, but for a growing group it is a hugely rewarding way of working, offering a degree of flexibility, creative control and shared endeavour unmatched by other models.

What follows is an exploration of the practice of five musical directors who have been associated with this work both in the UK and USA. Sarah Travis is a Tony Award winning musical director and arranger, whose long-standing collaborations with director John Doyle include the Broadway and West End productions of *Sweeney Todd*, she has also created a range of work in the UK including the national tours of *Fiddler on the Roof* and *Chess* with director Craig Revel Horwood. Paddy Cunneen's work as an MD and composer has included actor-musician productions at Liverpool Everyman, London's Donmar Warehouse and the National Theatre. He has worked on Broadway and the West End including creating the music for *Shakespeare in Love* and Sam Mendes' *Cabaret*, which both used actor-musicians to notable effect. Catherine Jayes, another long-time collaborator with John Doyle, has worked with actor-musicians since the 1980s when she MDed and arranged his groundbreaking production of *Candide* at Liverpool Everyman. She has gone on to work with a range of directors including Nikolai Foster, on actor-musician productions which include the 2014 UK tour of *Calamity Jane* and the Watermill's extraordinary 2001 reworking of Bizet's *Carmen*. Like many of our contributors she has also worked on high-profile mainstream musical theatre productions on stage and film including Tim Burton's movie version of *Sweeney Todd* and the critically acclaimed *Merrily We Roll Along* directed by Maria Friedman at London's Menier Chocolate Factory. Greg Palmer has been associated with actor-musicianship since 1988 when he worked at the Liverpool Everyman. He then went on to champion the form, creating a body of work that includes work for Stoke's New Vic Theatre, the Bubble, Century Theatre, Theatr Clwyd and Ipswich's New Wolsey, forming close working relationships with a range of leading directors of actor-musicianship including Peter Rowe, Bob Eaton and Hans Duijvendak. Finally Ben Goddard, who as an actor-musician has thrilled audiences on both sides of the Atlantic as Jerry Lee Lewis in the 2013 rock'n'roll actor-musician musical *Million Dollar Quartet*. His work as an MD includes a string of rock'n'roll pantomimes and new work for actor-musicians including the 2014 *Midsummer Songs* which he co-wrote with Peter Rowe.

A forgiving form

I think that theatre is quite a forgiving form for music insofar as a simple tune, which you might find cloying if heard in isolation, could be devastating within the context of a scene. You have more license to be simple, to be raw. It can accommodate such a range of musical approaches, even playing that in other settings might be regarded as poor. I did a show in Ireland which had a badly played fiddle in it, but it somehow suited the character and it had a life which the theatricality gives license to. (Paddy Cunneen)

While the ambition in much actor-musician work is to reflect the levels of musical sophistication provided by professional musicians, it is perhaps useful to begin with Paddy Cunneen's reminder of how the dramatic context guides an audience and informs their reception of music. Cunneen reminds us that music is only part of a matrix of meanings that include narrative setting, the physical and visual elements and in the case of actor-musicianship, the act of performance itself. In that sense actor-musicians are using music as only one element of their expression, in a way not replicated by pit bands or the presence of specialist musicians. This does not mean that one has to expect a lowering of musical standards, for in many cases actor-musicians with the advantage of a full rehearsal process rather than the pressure of a two-day band call can achieve very strong musical results, but rather that what actor-musicians have to offer is something different.

We all know that actor-musicians are a complete sensory thrill. You are being stimulated visually and aurally ... their talents are multi and they don't suit sitting and recording an album. For actor-musicians it is the feast of seeing them do what they do. Music is part of it, but it is a complete physical event. (Catherine Jayes)

It is this embracing of the 'multi', as Jayes puts it, that unites those who have contributed to this chapter. The actor-musician's identity as an actor offers a freshness in their approach to music-making, born perhaps out of the sheer joy of making music; a chance for them to indulge a passion and skill that is not their primary professional focus:

It has always been my experience that actor-musicians, given that they trained as actors and not musicians, get a big buzz out of making a piece of music because they are actually doing something that they enjoy and never thought they would get a chance to do at this level; especially a chance to get paid to do it. I quite often get people saying to me that they can't believe they are getting paid to do this and have so much fun as well. I think that sense creates a buzz between me as the MD and leader of the session and those involved. (Greg Palmer)

For some this difference in focus represents a compromise. The likes of Paul Gemignani and Jonathan Tunick, for example, have avoided working with actor-musicians, as Catherine Jayes suggested, because perhaps they are a particular breed of 'perfectionist musician', for whom the musical reworking required in actor-musicianship represents a reduction in scope and scale. For the right temperament, however, the musical direction of actor-musician work offers an opportunity for creative release and ownership, encouraging bravery as Sarah Travis puts it and collaboration like no other MDing context.

Multiple roles: The MD-orchestrator

Every actor-musician show I have ever done I have orchestrated. I would find it hard to come in and just MD. That is not to say that I can't or wouldn't want to collaborate with someone else, but it is just always the way that I have worked, so for me they are inseparable. (Sarah Travis)

MDs working on extant musicals with actor-musicians are engaged in an act of reinvention or at the very least reinterpretation. Whether in response to a reduction in musical forces or skill levels or as a reaction to new conceptual framings, MDing actor-musicianship frequently requires orchestrating or arranging skills. While this might be within the reach of most capable musical directors, it is important to note that these are usually seen as distinct disciplines in mainstream musical theatre practice, a fact reflected in the Tony Award categories, which include an award for best orchestration and a single award for best conductor and musical director. Given that actor-musicianship does not require a conductor, Sarah Travis' 2005 Tony was awarded for her orchestrations of *Sweeney Todd*. In actor-musicianship it seems, the act of MDing, like the act of performance, requires the harnessing of a dual skillset.

> In actor-musicianship you just don't know where the line exists, because how the stuff is being played on stage has such an impact on the music. There are so many cross-overs ... Before we even cast I have my orchestration-hat on to consider what instruments we might need to achieve the setting or style we are after. Then you go into the audition process and you are looking for a balance of the right voice, acting and instruments and things may change again. I always remember when we were casting for *Sweeney,* Rebecca [Jenkins] and David Ricardo Pearce both came in on the same day and played wonderful cello, and we came up with this idea of both the lovers playing the same instrument. That sort of happy accident often happens in auditions, so you cannot separate the process of MDing and orchestrating at that stage and it carries on throughout rehearsals. One minute I'll be teaching a vocal or instrumental line and within the teaching I can be re-orchestrating; I might be changing key or getting them to sing in a slightly different way. So for me you have to keep orchestrating as you MD in actor-musician work and that is the biggest difference I think. It can be tortuous, but it is joyous too. (Sarah Travis)

The approach to orchestration and arranging varies tremendously, but in all cases it is informed by the need to adapt to the varying needs of the actor-musician process.

> I will score something really thick knowing that things are gradually going to be taken away ... I like orchestrating for pit bands,

but that is more scary in a way, because at least with an actor-musician show I have four or five weeks to actually hear it and play and refine it. With a pit band I have two band calls and that is much more scary as you have to get it right straightaway. (Sarah Travis)

Travis' over-scoring enables her to strip back parts in response to changes in the rehearsal room. She uses a computer programme to generate her arrangements, which also allows her to transpose music into different keys and registers with relative ease. Catherine Jayes, by contrast, as I discovered when I was given the job of working as her assistant and copyist, produces the most beautiful hand-written orchestrations. The process of orchestration for Jayes is the creative starting point and one that her long-term collaborator John Doyle honours:

John was always very reverent to my musical arrangements. We were pretty pre-organised in those days; although there was always a sense of freedom in the room John is incredibly set-out before he starts. You always feel that he is making it up as he is going along and that is true to an extent, but he is always very well thought through and I don't think we changed very much musically at all.

There is still a need for a degree of flexibility, however, as Jayes goes on to describe:

On a purely practical level, you have to be able to adapt to the process and that requires the ability to change things. Nikolai [Foster] on *Calamity* liked to change things as we went along and so I had to double up parts to accommodate that possibility. I would have two or three people on the same guitar line because I knew it would happen much more with him and we needed to be flexible enough to allow for that.

In many instances, however, Jayes' experience of working with actor-musicians allows her to tailor the arrangements to the form, anticipating the physical discoveries that might occur in the rehearsal room and offering orchestrations that are informed by and suggestive of performance choices:

> If someone is playing a leading part and they are singing I love to get them to play as well, that is if they are string players or pianists. I think audiences love the feeling of an actor accompanying themselves, because you can express yourself so much on a instrument. When we did *Merrily We Roll Along* as an actor-musician show, Jo the cellist sang 'Not A Day Goes By' accompanying herself on the cello and what made it so moving to me was that she was playing too; her heart was going through her bow. You have to pick your songs for that and pick them so that the actor isn't compromised, but cellos and violins are just an extension of the body and soul really and so it is just wonderful when that dual expression happens. When she sang in anger it was brilliant, the cello was great for that. I knew how the anger could inform the cello part. You need to make it so that it does not feel oppositional, it has to feel as if it is part of what they are doing as a character.

As Paddy Cunneen suggests the 'forgiving' nature of the form means that the physical presence of the music can offer a context that supports even the simplest of musical choices. In Jayes' reimagining of the arrangements for *Calamity Jane,* for example, there is a moment that prompted Steve Oliver to write the following in his review for the *Nottingham Post*:

> Casting actor-musicians was another brilliant move, with a special mention for Tom Lister (Wild Bill Hickok) whose solo rendition of 'Higher Than A Hawk' on guitar is hairs-raised-on-the-back-of-your-neck stunning.[1]

This, as Jayes reflects, was a perfect example of how the act of orchestration can be altered by the presence of the instruments:

> There is a big ballad in *Calamity Jane* where a character accompanies himself on guitar and that is all there is and ironically that is the moment that everyone is talking about and yet all he is playing is chords on a guitar. It was the easiest thing that I had to do, but it is the thing that people related to the most. When you have a high emotional moment that is when self-accompaniment works best.

For Greg Palmer the impetus for and degree of orchestration and arranging varies according to the type of production and musical style. Palmer, although receiving a formal classical training as a pianist, has a rich musical background having played everything from new-wave punk to ceilidh music in a varied career as a professional musician. He combines a strong ability to improvise and play by ear with a formal musical knowledge to create musical arrangements that emerge from the rehearsal process, with very little orchestration undertaken in advance. Working with Palmer is a thrilling affair as he generates the music in the moment and in response to the people and skills in front of him, an approach made possible by the nature of the actor-musician rehearsal process, which allows the music to be discovered as part of the organic flow of rehearsals rather than being pre-planned and organized in preparation for a limited and last-minute band call. For Palmer this act of reinvention is prompted by a balance of the musical identity of the cast and the needs of the piece:

> It depends on the style of the music involved. If we are doing a straight musical with a score we will work from those charts, but almost always we don't have the exact forces that that particular production requires and so it requires a lot of rearranging, which could be as simple as putting a trumpet line on a clarinet, but when we are working in styles that tend not to have written musical information like folk or pop, then that information is usually just

sitting in my head. I have a pretty good understanding of musical shape and the forces I have got available to me and so then I will craft an arrangement based on my experience of listening and working with people ... the complexity of the orchestration and arrangement is guided by the skills of those people in front of you and for me that is a constantly fluctuating situation. It can even be led by something that somebody plays inadvertently in a rehearsal – someone might get a musical flight of fancy and play something and if I think that will improve or add to what we have then I will accommodative it in the arrangement. It is a two-way process that allows the cast to feel that they have some ownership over what is taking place ... I always have a starting point in terms of the sound I am after, but whether we actually stay there is another matter, it really does depend on what happens in the room.

Whether manifest in the preproduction process or a response to discoveries made in the room, the actor-musician MD must honour the intentions of the composer and the rigours of the music, while facilitating the synergy of music-making in performance. The range of skills found in the cast and the chamber-like quality of much actor-musician work requires a hybrid approach that marries the knowledge of theatre and narrative found in the mainstream musical theatre MD, with the ability to adapt and work with the needs of musicians more typically found in rock, pop and folk band settings. This type of player is used to a musical environment governed by the collective endeavour of the band and the ebb and flow of the music they create, rather than the rigour of reading a score, where musical shape and form is prescribed. The role of arranger and orchestrator as an extension of the MDing process is, therefore, an essential outcome of actor-musicianship as a music-making process.

Perhaps we can end this section with a comment from Sarah Travis that reminds us of how musical sensibilities must ultimately govern the MD's approach, balanced, as we have outlined, with the possibilities suggested by integrated musicianship:

When I score shows I am not interested in how many instruments I can get in, which I think was almost part of the form in the past, 'So and so can play ten instruments so let's use as many as we can'. It became an 'aren't we clever?' sort of thing. Unless it is absolutely necessary I am not interested in swapping. I notice swaps musically unless they are done really well.

At its best actor-musician work can sound exquisite. Martin Lowe's work on *Once*, for example, is some of the finest sounding music to be heard in the theatre both in terms of his arrangements and the quality of the musicianship. As *Once* so beautifully demonstrates, however, the music in actor-musicianship has to be conceived as a multi-sensory event, reliant not just on the sound, but the way music is moulded to the physical life of the piece and its narrative content. The blending of arranging and MDing is part of that process, so too is the approach to rehearsal and working with the actor-musician as performer.

Managing the room: Approaches to rehearsals

Seasoned professional musicians work in such a way that they are confronted with a set of dots, they have a particular timescale in which they are expected to come up with the goods and that is what their training has led them towards, where as with an actor-musician the emphasis is very different. (Greg Palmer)

Music is frequently the starting point in rehearsals for actor-musician musicals. The music must be embedded before other layers can be explored. In turn the process of learning the music becomes a point of focus for the members of the creative team, whether that be director, choreographer, lighting or sound designers; a chance for them to begin to explore ways in which the music and music-making will inform their processes. The actor-musician music rehearsal as a result is a pivotal moment for all involved, a moment led and managed by the musical director.

> There is a lot that is the same, when I am rehearsing actor-musicians. In a music call I rehearse them like a pit band. We sit round and we rehearse as I would in any band call, but I feel able to change things more with actor-musicians, whereas with a band it is much harder because you have a level of pressure due to time and the fact that it is often at the end of the process. (Catherine Jayes)

As Catherine Jayes suggests in many ways the actor-musician band call is not unlike a music rehearsal for specialist musicians; what is different however is its context and culture. It has all the hallmarks of a regular band call: the company is usually seated, particularly in the early stages of rehearsal; there will be music stands with music or chord sheets on them; a configuration that promotes the making of music, usually a semi-circle that facilitates listening and visual cues; the MD will frequently occupy the central position traditionally reserved for the conductor. What differs, however, is that as the MD looks out he or she sees simultaneously both cast and orchestra. Behind each music stand there is a musician, actor and character. Added to this is the very particular mix of anxiety and excitement that the actor-musician feels as they approach the making of music. As Greg Palmer reminds us these are not 'seasoned professional musicians':

> You are working with actors principally and the musical experiences of those actors will be as wide and varied as you can possibly imagine. You will be dealing with some people who are tied to dots and on the other hand there are those who may never have read a piece of music in their lives and you have to find a way of working with those people and then find a way of making those different types communicate with each other through the musical

experience ... there might be people with whom you have worked previously and others who you will almost certainly have auditioned and will have a rough idea of what their skills are, but you don't really know until you get them into the rehearsal room how quick they are at assimilating information: whether they can pick up a rhythm or what their sense of time is like. (Greg Palmer)

The actor-musician MD has to be adaptable, their teaching and nurturing skills must be finely tuned. They need to be sensitive to the various approaches in the room, of the fact that the company will contain people from 'all musical walks of life' as Ben Goddard put it. Unlike the uniform approach of the specialist musician the needs of each cast member differs, informed by instrument, levels of skill and musical confidence and by their role within the production. Someone with a large responsibility within the dramatic action, for example, will have less capacity to take on musical information and may be less available to play depending on the nature of the show or the taste and governing aesthetic of the production. Central to the process is the realization that, although these early music calls may be facilitated by the use of sheet music or chord sheets, the show will eventually be played from memory; the exception being the first keyboard player who can sometimes get away with having music in performance:

The important distinction is that we almost always ask our actor-musicians to learn the music. That produces a different sense in the performer. Occasionally you will find people who have come from those formal modes and if they are suddenly put in the position of having to work without dots or learn music then that can put them in a bit of a funk ... You simply have to make it plain at the outset that this is what we are working towards and facilitate a process that allows them to learn the music. Their training as actors, which has taught them to learn lines and be able to reproduce them on stage without reference to script, helps them

to do the same with music. I am sure there is a connection there
somehow. (Greg Palmer)

As Sarah Travis reminds us, however, this does not mean that musical
precision and rigour has to be abandoned, as the high level of her
actor-musician practice suggests:

> I very rarely simplify stuff, but if there is a passage that is slightly
> different in repeat then I might regulate that in order to help them
> with the learning process. And just drilling – getting something on
> its feet as early as possible so that it becomes part of their body as
> soon as it can be because it is a very technical process, inevitably
> they have to input the notes, the text and movement into their
> bodies and memory so the earlier you can get everything working
> together the better.

Again the approach is tempered by the nature of the production
and company. Like Sarah Travis, Catherine Jayes' work has been
predominantly on extant musicals adapted for actor-musicians. For
her the demands of this sort of music, coupled with the expectation of
audiences and a rise in the range and proficiency of actor-musicians
over the years has meant that often the very highest musical
standards can be achieved:

> I think I used to make rather simplistic arrangements, because in
> those early days I was terribly conscious of what one was throwing
> at people, but of course now I would never think that. I would
> orchestrate as I would for a pit band. There are people who are
> now so good that you can write anything for them ... In *Calamity*
> I've got a banjo player who understands the musical style of the
> show and he will play licks that he creates, I will say I can write
> these, but I am not a banjo player so I ask him what he would
> do with the idea. And that is the same as working with profes-
> sional musicians, you might say to a guitarist 'I've got this chord

sequence, can you do something around that?' It is often more interesting than the music I would make and it means they become creative artists too.

For many MDs the need to achieve a full and complex score in a relatively short time means that the actor-musicians must be able to read music, even if they have then to commit it to memory for performance:

> It is so dependent on what the project is. If you are doing *Sweeney Todd* or *Fiddler on the Roof* in the time we have, then you need to have people who can read. Guitars are different as they can work from chords, but anything else you need to be able to read to do that sort of work. I haven't got time to teach aurally. Even in *The Hired Man*, which we did with young people, they all read – I would very seldom write something specific, but I would give them the chord structure and then work with them to shape what they could offer in response. When you are working with brass, woodwind and strings, however, I just couldn't do it. They don't need to be virtuosic; if they can take parts away and in their own way learn it that is great, but I think they need to be able to play something in that first rehearsal because I have to be able to hear it. If I give someone a clarinet part and it is two days before they can play it, then it is too late because in that first call I need to start to play around with things. I want to be able to hear the music quite early. It is the voicing of sections that you really need to hear. So I think the bar is quite high now and you do need to be able to read. (Sarah Travis)

To read or not to read is certainly a pertinent question for MDs working with and casting actor-musicians. Confidence levels and musical standards and approaches may vary within cast groups, but when approaching complex scores Catherine Jayes shares many of Sarah Travis' concerns:

On *Calamity Jane* I had guitarists and they all read something whether that be chords or music, except one who did play by ear, but I didn't notice he couldn't read because he would just go off and learn it. We only had four weeks to put on a musical with choreography, which is a tall order. They were pretty good readers and the ones that weren't just worked really hard at it, because they were intimidated by the musical skills of others and that is something that you don't want in a show. You don't want that sense of imbalance.

As we discovered in earlier chapters the history of actor-musicianship is deeply rooted in the populist, working-class theatre movements of Joan Littlewood and John McGrath. For them and the likes of Glen Walford and those early Bubble and Everyman companies, there was something powerful about the rough-and-ready approach to music-making that resonated with their audiences. As actor-musicianship has matured, however, so the skill-set of those it attracts has developed, presenting a very different set of challenges to MDs, as Ben Goddard explains:

The world has moved on. It isn't what it was like when they started doing *Planet* back in the 1980s. It isn't the case that companies say, 'we are just a bunch of actors who play a few instruments, some of us are really brilliant musically, but you've never played bass so here have a go'. It is not like that any more ... Lots of actor-musicians are serious musicians these days and when you have got people like that in the room it feels like you are short-changing the experience by having someone who has never played the trumpet before and is just 'having a go'. These days the skills have increased because of the success of the shows from the Watermill. You have to be a really strong musician to be able to pull off the score of *Sweeney Todd* or *Sunset Boulevard* and that has worked its way back. So when you go back to the rock'n'roll shows like I do, you now have that same level of skill and I have come to expect that. I have no need to take someone who hasn't played the bass guitar before when I know I can hire a highly skilled bass player who can do it correctly. The level has got so high … You just can't turn up knowing a few chords and say I play guitar, that just doesn't work anymore.

The standard of musicianship may well be high, but for Goddard the varied approaches to music-making found in most actor-musician companies still informs his approach to rehearsals:

When I first started MDing rock 'n' roll shows I would have the arrangements in my head and I would just show people how they went, in a largely aural process. I found it was relatively easy for me to go to a guitarist and show him how a chord progression might go, but the people who played brass, who would often come from a classical training background, would take longer to learn it that way, simply because they are not used to working like that, they are used to reading off a page. So now what I do is score everything, mainly because of the constraints of time and also because it means everyone has got a score as a point of reference. So even if you are a guitarist who doesn't know what the dots mean, you can still read the chord symbols at the top and see which order they go in. It is just a way of unifying a group of people with widely differing skill-sets and it saves time, which is what it is often about. You have three weeks to get through 28 songs and that is incredibly tight. That for me is the main skill for an MD of actor-musicianship – to be able to work with people from all walks of musical life.

The flexibility required of MDs working with actor-musicians extends to readers and non-readers alike, individuals may be cast for their acting or dance ability or because they are just right for the part because of age or physical type. The musical requirements have to be considered as only a part of the whole, as Greg Palmer reflects:

I do still take non-readers. It depends on the show, but again it is all about the level of collaboration required in these processes, quite often directors or choreographers will want people for another skill set that they have, so it does not and often cannot be about working exclusively with readers. I don't think that will ever be the case. I know fantastic actor-musicians who do not read, but they have wonderful skills that we can harness. It is just about finding a different way of communicating with them. It is great if actors can read music, but it is not the only way, it never was, it isn't now and it never will be.

Paddy Cunneen reminds us that although approaches to learning and facilitating actor-musician music-making may need to encompass readers and those who do not read music, there is fundamentally something more important and interesting that underpins the process:

I think being able to read is the manifestation of a sensibility and not the sensibility itself and I am interested in working with the sensibility. Ultimately it is about the experience of consuming the music together in that moment, whether you are reading it or not is irrelevant. If you have an actor-musician who has to learn the music without reading, then there is already a level of passionate engagement. That actor-musician is already engaged and all I ever really want is engagement … . What we do works within a professional context and of course it is worth encouraging anyone to learn to read even a little bit, because it gives you a more professional edge, but it is not what you do. Tim Van Eyken came in to audition, for example, for *Shakespeare in Love* and he played his flute with such conviction and appeal that of course we wanted him and we asked if he could be the MD and he said 'but I don't read'. And we said, 'that's alright, we can sort all that' because what is more important is to have somebody at the centre of the group who is providing leadership not through notational accuracy, but through feel. You want the feel to be right … You wouldn't say that somebody isn't a poet because they are not able to write it down because the art of being a poet is to have that something within you that resonates and bursts into this extraordinary thing now and again and makes the world more magical and clearer in the way that poetry does.

For Cunneen it is the actor's imagination that MDs of actor-musicianship must harness in the music-making process:

I don't care about getting the notes right I care about the inspiration that generates the notes. I care about what makes it transcendent. I encourage actor-musicians to not get it right, but to play with an extreme sensitivity to the scene and I would struggle to get that out of a musician, but the actor-musician understands that … Quite often it's about an acceptance that the dynamic must be incredibly low, which feels demeaning in some respects: for a musician to constantly be told 'play more quietly' they feel deflated, but for an actor-musician actually they do just enough for the action to take place. They see it the other way round.

It is this embracing of the actor within the process of music-making that perhaps best characterizes the approach to MDing actor-musicianship:

My sympathy for actor-musicians goes towards their acting, I want the music to be right, but if I watch it and I think they have lost something in the acting then I feel saddened because that is much harder to maintain than a quick fix to the music. Again it is to do with the forgiving nature of theatre because of its multi-sensory dimension. It is not just about the sound, but about the emotional life of the actor – that is what we all want to see isn't it? Then the picking up of the instrument becomes almost incidental, it is not the main thing that we are tuned in to. The thrill for the audience is getting enraptured by the actor and then forgetting that they are playing … That is the thing that seems to have developed over the years, this idea of making the instrument part of the emotional meaning rather than just a visual thing, because of course the visual is very tantalizing and inventive. The instrument can become something else: a prop or a child. I think the emotional emphasis is my preferred way of working on these shows. (Catherine Jayes)

The sense of collective endeavour actor-musicianship engenders, informs and delights MDs that work in this field. The process enables a level of discovery and ownership that Paddy Cunneen encapsulates:

I think one of the great things about actor-musicianship is that it enables me to go into the rehearsal room uncluttered with ideas that I would be imposing on the production. I always prefer to go in and be exposed to the process like an actor might be and to learn what the production is and to grow the musical ideas in conjunction with the emerging production ideas and with actor-musicians you can do that much more easily. And so conceptually there is a big advantage to it. You don't have to solve all your musical problems in advance.

It allows MDs to work in an organic manner, responding to the moment both sonically and in their approach to the music-making. Unlike mainstream musical theatre processes the MD of the actor-musician show gets to hear the music as they go along, allowing them to shape and craft arrangements in tandem with the process of rehearsing the action. Music calls, particularly at the early stages of rehearsal, are a chance to find a collective sound and to adapt arrangements to the needs of the group and the piece; for creative teams to hear the fully realized sonic world of the production, informing the direction of the piece as a whole. As contributors have hinted, however, there comes a point when the company must bring the music into the stage action. The nature of the performance aesthetic will mitigate this process, but in many productions musical staging, choreography and the needs of story can lead to music-making taking a back seat, at least for a while.

> These days you can get casts who can sight read or are familiar enough with the music to enable a really strong play-through even at first rehearsal, but the car-crash moment is always the first staging session. (Sarah Travis)

This can happen in the rehearsal room as a company first attempts to integrate music into a danced section, or at the point when the show moves into the theatre; the change of acoustic and physical distance between instruments leading to a break-down in musical communication. The results can sound very unpleasant. This 'car-crash moment' is often quite unnerving for inexperienced casts and MDs. It is, however, impossible to keep all plates spinning all the time and so there inevitably comes a point when the MD has to let go of the musical imperatives to facilitate other areas of the actor-musician's work:

> I sort of like those moments now because you know what is happening. I know that the music will get back in the end, you just have to trust that they will get there and part of my job is to nurture them through the scary time of putting it together. They fear that they will never be able to learn it all, but people do. We have an incredible capacity and once it is up on its feet it is a lot easier because it becomes part of the whole for the actor. (Sarah Travis)

MDs working with actor-musicians have to be sensitive to the range of skills required in performance and to their primary identity as actors. The finite nature of music-making means that the risk of being wrong is greater than in acting processes and that fear of risk has always been the enemy of good art. MDs have to embrace and support the essential vulnerability that actors feel when working with music. As Catherine Jayes reflects the process of actor-musicianship is arguably the most exposing of all performance forms:

What is interesting is that actor-musicians can feel quite bare if they don't have their instrument with them and I will sometimes put in a couple of phrases just to enable them to have their instrument at that moment ... the instrument can be a shield, but generally speaking the stronger the connection between the actor, the voice and the instrument the stronger the sense of vulnerability. All these things are interconnected. I remember Judi Dench was interviewed by Richard Eyre about press intrusion in her private life, which she found intolerable because for her the process of acting is so revealing in itself. Now when someone is also singing and playing an instrument for goodness' sake, that is about as exposed as you can get.

Working without a conductor

One of the defining elements of actor-musicianship as a musical process is the absence of the conductor. Part of its visceral appeal is the very direct connection between music, storytelling and audience, unfettered by the presence of the mediating force of the conductor. It contains an element of risk. How will they keep together? What if they forget their music? Who is in charge? This risk is part of the frisson of the work, for audiences and companies alike. Actor-musicians enjoy controlling their own musical destiny, having the chance to shape every aspect of their storytelling, but it is a dangerous business and one that belies the very necessary input and skill of the MD, whose job it is to instill tempo and musical shape as part of the rehearsal process; remaining powerless once the show is in performance.

Inevitably after a couple of weeks when people are confident with what they are playing the tempos will always go faster and often if I come back and see the show I have to rein it in, because one tempo will have an effect on the next and so it goes on. I think that tempos in actor-musician shows are the hardest thing to get right. (Sarah Travis)

To a certain extent it is wrong to characterize actor-musicianship as conductorless, for there is often a dominant or leading force built into the arrangements or negotiated as part of the rehearsal process:

> You just have to work really hard in rehearsals to try and ensure that everyone knows where the pulse needs to be and obviously it is a liquid thing. Even when things are set very strict there is always a slight degree of up and down in terms of tempo, but it requires an awful lot of coaching, that is probably one of the trickiest aspects of it. I try to tailor the arrangements to enable those tempo shifts to happen as smoothly as they can. I might, for example, try to reduce the arrangement so that there were not quite so many people involved. Even so there can be some pretty tricky moments. When we did *Guy and Dolls,* for example, it was a bit like an ocean liner that takes three or four miles to slow down because of its size. I think we had something like 22 instrumentalists, so trying to find a way of negotiating a tempo change, like a sudden ral and a pick up, depended on one or two of that company guiding everyone through. That could be with a hand gesture, but more often than not their hands were occupied, so it might just be a raised eyebrow, a nod of the head or a move of the shoulder, but it is tricky. (Greg Palmer)

MDs must build these considerations into their process, whether that be within the arranging or facilitating of music in the rehearsal room, as Catherine Jayes highlights:

> I might start a number with just one player, just in case sight lines are such that a group of players can't see each other. Beginnings and ends of numbers need to be considered in this way particularly. But often directors will need to react to the musical needs,

adapting the staging to enable the music-making and facilitate sight lines.

Actor-musician companies operate like bands, they are self-determining and musically autonomous; however, the MD has to find ways of creating a sustainable shape that reflects the choices made in the rehearsal room and that honours the dramaturgy contained in the music. For Ben Goddard it is the knowledge of how bands operate that informs this approach:

I came from a very disciplined musical background as a child, practising for seven or eight hours a day, but then as a teenager I discovered Led Zeppelin and girls and all I wanted to do was be in a band. So my skill as an MD has always been informed by how to put a band together, but I am not just doing that in the sense of 'let's just get into a room and vibe it out'. I always come in with the same discipline that I got from the classical world ... It requires real musicianship and close listening skills. When you don't have a conductor there has to be an inner engine that comes from all of you ... someone always kind of leads, which is what often happens in a band, the drums and bass are often driving it. But there is a collective concentration between all those on stage that means you can speed up and slow down as a unit. As an MD you can give an instruction like 'you must drive through these next ten bars' and they do. Now at first it may be a bit of a bun fight, but then they start playing as a band, as opposed to as an orchestra, and that is really exciting. It's like those moments in a rowing boat when you are all pulling the same way, but you are not quite working at the same time and the boat is rocky, then suddenly you are all in sync; there is no one calling it out, you just start to feel each other and suddenly the boat is flying. It is the same in an actor-musician show. There is no one person taking responsibility, it is a collective understanding, a true ensemble feel. And that is why I love the work more than anything it really does feel like everyone pulling in the same direction and that is the most exciting feeling of all.

Once again the very particular connection to narrative and emotional contexts that actor-musicians have access to can be helpful in finding and sustaining tempo. This requires the MD to draw on language that is perhaps more usually regarded as the territory of the director, as Sarah Travis describes:

> My job is often about getting them to emotionally connect when they are playing and that often is about tempo. If I start clapping or clicking a beat I am clapping my interpretation of what the emotional content of that moment is. I think that is hard because it is my interpretation and not theirs. As a musician I don't analyse moments like that I just feel them, but it is important to instil that in the music ... It is so hard because one beat-per-minute can make all the difference, it is so subjective, someone might be feeling that moment differently from someone else and that is what is so wonderful about the actor-musician process; it encourages a collective sense of feeling. Those are the moments that really come alive in the rehearsal room, when the tempo comes naturally because the whole company is in the same place emotionally, but that is hard to recreate every night so there needs to be a safeguard.

That safeguard can often be a visual cue from a lead instrument such as the keyboard player or rhythm section. In this sense actor-musicianship is perhaps best served by the intimacy of the chamber-style or small venues such as the Watermill. With her shows now touring to number-one venues and large concert halls, however, Travis has found a need for interventions that enable this process:

> In *Chess* and *Fiddler* a camera was the only solution because of the set and those big touring spaces. At the Watermill we didn't

need it because everyone could see and feel each other, but on those big stages I think you need help, unless it is a very confined set. You just need to be able to see someone nodding-in the beginning of numbers and that was all the camera was needed for on that show, there was no conducting to keep people in time apart from a few moments that were very *rubato*. In *Sweeney* we did not have cameras, but we did have a mirror mounted on the piano because the pianist was facing upstage, enabling him to see the company. In *Chess* I even had a screen above the stage facing down because there was a number when they were lying down and on that show I had an offstage pianist and he did conduct a lot of it, but there were just so many of them in that show that it needed it. But ideally I wouldn't use any cameras and I wouldn't want keyboards off stage.

However it is achieved the MD of actor-musicianship must facilitate the formation of a band and facilitate the handing over of control of the music to them. It is not a job for the faint of heart or for those for whom control is an ambition or pleasure. As with so much actor-musician practice it is about engaging with the collective endeavour:

In a lot of theatre it is about 'when is my bit?' But in these shows it is always about 'us'. From day one I rehearse the band so they never just play their bit, but they play 'us'. The proudest moment for me is when I see them all looking at each other and communicating, when they play as one company. You have to set that up early. (Ben Goddard)

Collaboration

Directors either think that they shouldn't involve themselves in the music because it is not their role or because they think they don't have enough specialist knowledge, but it is really important that they do because that is when ideas will spark. (Sarah Travis)

The level and nature of collaboration in actor-musician practice has been something of a running theme in this book and there is no escaping it in relation to the role of musical director. As we have already established the levels of overlap even extend to the amalgamation of roles such as MD and orchestrator. It would be foolish to assume that other areas of theatre practice do not contain examples of collaborative practice, but what is unavoidable in the case of actor-musicianship is that the result are always improved when a more fluid approach to discipline-specific specialty is adopted. This might be defined as the need for a stronger directorial approach to MDing or the encouragement of directorial engagement with musical processes. One thing is certain – the dual skill set of the performers requires a level of collaboration between the creative team, simply because of the practical concerns that govern the making of the work. Pre-production meetings have to extend to detailed discussions between director and MD about how the music is going to be facilitated. They are after all calling on the same group of performers, which affects both the casting and orchestrating process:

Usually when I am working with Pete [Rowe] we will talk in a reasonably detailed manner about what forces are available to us and I will read the script with an eye on who is available to me to produce the score and there is often a bit of toing and froing about who might be available to play. (Greg Palmer)

This process requires a distinctive approach to pre-production. MDs of actor-musician shows must read the script not simply to provide narrative context for the music, but to identify when and how their band members might be available to play:

I am reading the script and looking at who is available. If there are eight out of a cast of 12 on stage and I have to produce a fanfare

> that is going to announce the arrival of a prince in the next scene
> and my two trumpeters are among those eight, then I am going to
> have to find another way of doing it or I need to talk to the director
> about how we might solve that particular problem … It is a big
> administrative task, I had to use spreadsheets for shows like *Guys
> and Dolls* detailing who is where at any given point in the story, but
> usually I scribble detailed notes in my script, so I know who has
> gone off-stage in time to be able to pick up their trumpet as part
> of the next cue. (Greg Palmer)

Once rehearsals are under way the lines of communication must
remain fluid. Rehearsal schedules are frequent areas of conflict – with
MDs needing to ensure that time is allowed for band calls to support
the process of integration. I have too often seen directors winning this
battle, resulting in band calls happening in the evenings only or as an
extension of warm-ups. Similarly MDs can sometimes be too keen
to work independently, forgetting the need for integration of stage
action. As always it is a constant balancing act. When choreography
is required the matrix of collaboration extends further, as Catherine
Jayes found when working with choreographer Nick Winston:

> *Calamity* was an interesting job because the tempi of things was
> dictated by the choreographer much more than I was expecting. I
> have always ruled the musical roost on an actor-musician musical
> show, but tempi was very much part of Nick's [Winston] domain.

Sarah Travis encountered similar issues in her collaborations with
Craig Revel Horwood who is both choreographer and director of his
actor-musician shows:

> With Craig and John [Doyle] I have a shorthand, but I also know
> where my battles are going to be and with Craig my battles are
> going to be in the moments of dance because he is a choreog-
> rapher at heart. We both laugh about it, but we know that there

will be conflicting needs. In *Fiddler* it was the bottle dance. He wanted dancing, but for a big dance number I need people to play and so inevitably we are going to have to barter and compromise. It is an eight minute piece and it needs to build musically and yet during the choreography session, which took an entire morning, he was gradually taking more and more people out of the musical line up to facilitate the dance. In the end I just had to say, 'Stop, no more! Please let Michael play the trumpet in this bit.' It was almost ridiculous. What you are trying to achieve is to tell the story in the best way you can both musically and in all other senses.

MDs of actor-musician shows may also need to work closely with designers to ensure that the physical elements of the music-making are facilitated, as Catherine Jayes describes:

I will mention that the instruments need to be kept somewhere safe, which often means lots of hooks on walls and places to put things. You are never as an MD in on the design processes, but you hope that the director and designer have thought that through. As an actor if you are changing from flute to clarinet you want it to be seamless.

It is the sound design of actor-musician shows, however, that is often the trickiest area for MDs to influence. As with so many aspects of the production process a deep understanding of the music-making process is necessary for a sound design that honours both the sound and the very particular physical demands of actor-musician shows:

You need a sound designer who understands actor-musicians, who will come in and watch two weeks of rehearsals, so he will almost be part of the band. The ideal sound designer comes and watches and listens and learns over a period of time. He knows the orchestrations as well as I do. Those who are not like that can become a nightmare to work with … An actor-musician show should be as acoustic as it dares to be so that all the sound is coming from the actors. The best actor-musician designers manage to make it sound like the sound is coming from the players. It is difficult especially in big spaces, but it is possible. You can't be irritated by the problems it throws up, you have to see them as part of the creative challenge. (Catherine Jayes)

Rights issues

Despite the creative freedom that actor-musician processes suggest for MDs, there is a need to be mindful of the performance rights issues that govern the use of composed music and orchestrations. This is a particularly grey area as actor-musicianship, as we have acknowledged, is often synonymous with the act of reinterpreting extant musical material. The recent high profile successes of shows like *Sweeney Todd* and their acceptance by living composers such as Stephen Sondheim have certainly made things easier, but still MDs of actor-musicianship have to navigate what can be the rather murky waters of performance rights:

It was all really scary. I remember the opening night of *Sweeney* at the Watermill, standing outside with John [Doyle], Jill [Fraser] and Richard [G. Jones] and saying: "Oh my God what have we done!" We didn't know what was going to happen with it, but there was a sense that we had taken a big risk ... Sometimes I have to sign a bit of paper which is quite scary, that can often mean that you do not own your arrangements. They become the property of the estate and sometimes they ask to see your orchestrations, often before you have even gone in to rehearsals. But I have never really had massive issues. I always feel that my job is to respect that composer and in certain scenarios to respect the original orchestrations. With *Fiddler*, for example, I was very aware of the rights issues and we didn't cut any of it. I was as true to the original orchestrations as possible, but certain estates simply won't allow you to do actor-musician versions of shows. (Sarah Travis)

In most instances the use of actor-musicians necessitates reinvention. The same can of course be true for productions that use specialist musicians. The financial constraints of many contemporary productions require a need for a reduction in the size or scale of band, which is akin to the musical changes necessary in actor-musicianship:

I have only really ever encountered rights issues with the [Kurt] Weill estate, who are very strict, but even then I have made the music work for whatever environment I have found myself in. I have done *The Threepenny Opera* three times now and each time with vastly different forces and on two of those occasions I had very limited forces and so I had to realize the music with just flute, piano and saxophone, so you just get on with it. (Greg Palmer)

As Catherine Jayes reminds us, however, it is not only the performing rights issues that can cause a problem when adapting music for actor-musician projects:

We did *Amadeus* and I was torn apart for that because they brought in music critics. I was so upset by that, because I am sure they sat and closed their eyes and just listened to the play. They were actor-musicians and I had re-orchestrated Mozart, I mean what an arrogance, but I was forced to by the nature of the show, and I have to say that the playwright Peter Shaffer loved the whole thing, but that was a difficult and challenging experience. I was having to rework symphonies and concertos for a small ensemble of actor-musicians. That was a lesson for me that actually sometimes you have to say no.

There may be trouble ahead

> Most theatre that is really gripping is a bit on the edge and actor-musicianship is at its best when it is pushing the boundaries or taking risks and at its worst when it begins to be stuck-on as a means to an end. It relies on a director and producer who can embrace the use of actor-musicians, rather than seeing them as a way of saving money. (Sarah Travis)

It is interesting that this chapter should end with a section that is so broadly focused. In one way it is a useful means of moving our discussion to a close, a chance to look at possible developments for this form of theatre making, but it is also reflective of a concern that came through in the meetings I had with MDs in preparation for this chapter. It seems that of all the practitioners who engage with actor-musicians, it is the MDs who feel most the injustice and exploitation that can characterize the worst of actor-musicianship. I guess as musicians themselves they are acutely aware of the perception that actor-musicians might be taking work from specialist musicians and therefore are keen for the performance context to present a clear argument for the duality of the performer. Here then are a series of quotes from some of our key contributors that offer the MD's perspective on how actor-musicianship may be taking a turn for the worst:

> I worry that there are too many actor-musician shows made because of financial imperatives. Too many being done for the wrong reasons. You don't want a group of actors being used as a cheap band. You want to see their work as part of the action. (Catherine Jayes)

> The problem with actor-musicians is that they are f**king clever and producers have worked it out. They have realized that it is

a way to not pay for an orchestra, so in some shows you see non-musical leading characters supported by a group of actors playing lesser parts and acting mainly as musicians. The moment you take away the idea of an ensemble that extends to every character on stage, then you have lost something. The moment you separate the principles from the ensemble, then that is not actor-musicianship. It is unfair to pit-musicians because it is taking work away from them and it is unfair to actor-musicians to be told that they are being employed as actors and then not being allowed to act. That just feels like a cheap way of doing a show. (Ben Goddard)

I am involved in the development of a new piece in America. It is a big production and there was to be a cast of about twenty-three and the casting breakdown is tiered: principals, featured actors, actor-musicians and musician-actors. I have never come across that before and so I keep asking what is the difference between an 'actor-musician' and a 'musician-actor' and they said, 'Well the actor-musicians are stronger actors and the musician-actors are stronger musicians.' I have never even thought of it like that before and I don't want to. In the end my heart just sank. They are down the bottom of the list and it just feels like it is being used a cheap option. (Sarah Travis)

As actor-musicianship becomes part of the mainstream it is only natural that it should be absorbed into the mechanisms that govern theatre making. Let us end this section on musical direction with this observation from Sarah Travis, which rather ironically illustrates how efforts to reduce the possible exploitation of actor-musicians may be reducing the capacity to work in ways that have historically enabled this practice to develop into a distinctive form. As has been observed in previous chapters, it is not always helpful to borrow models from specialist music practice when attempting to support and nurture actor-musicianship:

Union rules in America mean that there are now additional fees for doubling and trebling and so it is becoming as expensive to use actor-musicians who play multiple instruments as specialist musicians. During rehearsals I want to be able to feel that I can ask players to use another instrument. Actor-musician rehearsals have always been very organic affairs, but now it seems I may no longer be allowed to do that.

Note

1   Steve Oliver, review of *Calamity Jane* UK tour, *Nottingham Post*, 8 October 2014.

7
A YOUNG THEATRE

Over the last few years German theatre makers who specialize in work for young people have sought to escape the pejorative connotations that are frequently attached to the label 'children's theatre' by calling their work Young Theatre or '*Junges Theater*'.[1] For them this reflects both the nature of their target audience and the ambitions and history of the children's theatre movement, which has frequently been at the cutting edge of theatre practice. Theatre for young audiences has a wide remit, engaging audiences from 0–18 years of age, as UK based company Oily Cart's strap-line suggests, the company and sector as a whole are responsible for making 'all sort of shows, for all sorts of kids'. As a result of this breadth and in response to the openness of its audience, untarnished by understandings of established theatre conventions and the expectations they imply, the sector has often been at the vanguard of theatre making. Brian Way's Theatre Centre, founded in the 1960s in the UK, for example, was the first company to champion theatre-in-the-round, offering a more dynamic experience for school children watching in school halls, while reducing the need for large scenic elements which would be impractical to tour. So called 'baby-theatre' and work directed at pre-verbal or profoundly disabled children initiated the development of immersive, multi-sensory and non-narrative approaches to theatre making long before post-dramatic trends in mainstream adult-theatre took hold. As I alluded to in Chapter 1, some of the earliest uses of actor-musicians in the UK were also in theatre made for young audiences. Glen Walford's Bubble company and its predecessor Theatre Vanguard in Sheffield both made work for children, as did the Everyman and other companies identified with early actor-musician work such as Coventry's Belgrade theatre. Children and young people are important markers in the story of actor-musicianship for a number of reasons: first, they are an audience attuned to music in a way unlike their adult counterparts; second, they have engendered an approach to theatre making and performance that has embraced the inclusion and integration of music and music-making; third, they will themselves become the theatre makers, performers and audiences of the future. It will be their developing imaginations and creativity that will shape the future of our theatre culture.

Today's young people are arguably some of the most musically literate of any generation. The advent of the MP3 player and smartphone means that young people today have hundreds if not thousands of tracks available to them at any given time. Their tastes are eclectic with music of all genres available to download at the swipe of a touch-screen. It is young people who hold the key to the future of actor-musicianship and so it seems appropriate to end our enquiry by a brief look at how it has been shaped by them and to examine some of the indictors of where it might be going in their more-than-capable hands.

Children's musical culture

It was ethnomusicologist John Blacking who first coined the phrase 'children's musical culture'[2] in reference to his studies of the children of the Venda people of Western Africa. He identified that the music made by the children differed from that of the adult Venda. This analysis was to be the springboard for many future enquiries into the very particular relationship children and young people have to music and music-making, some, such as the work of Patricia Shehan

Campbell, using the methodology and framing offered by ethnomusicology, while others, such as the more recent work of Dr. Victoria Williamson, offering analysis from the field of music psychology. From both perspectives the outcomes are clear: children and young people have a distinctive and instinctual relationship to music.

In *Songs in their Heads*[3] Patricia Shehan Campbell offers a compelling account of just how complex and varied the musical output of children can be. Through observation of a range of children of varying ages and in various settings she provides an account and analysis of the role music and music-making plays in their everyday lives and interactions. She defines their music expression as 'musicking',[4] a term developed by Christopher Small to describe all human musical activity, from singing and playing an instrument through to rhythmic or musical movements and sounds. Campbell's observations range from the songs young children improvise in their day-to-day lives, through to the rhythmic movements and tapping that they display whilst waiting in the dinner queue or at mealtime. The book prompted me to notice just how musically creative my own children were. My four and five year old daughters tended to turn most activities into musical events; a repeated call to be taken to the toilet soon morphed into a musical chant 'I need a wee-wee, I need a pee-pee' and songs from the radio or theatre visits would be repeated, corrupted and developed to suit their own needs and as a reflection of their own psychological and emotional development. Victoria Williamson's 2014 book *You Are The Music*,[5] by contrast, offers a systematic look at the impact music has on the development of the brain and psychology of children, young people and adults. It maps the complex and deep-rooted ways in which music reflects and informs the development of intellectual, emotional and cultural traits. Indeed she provides evidence that reinforces the centrality of music to human communication and language:

The study by Brigit Mampe suggests that babies can not only perceive and remember the musical patterns of the speech they hear *in utero* but that they also mimic these familiar patterns when making their first cries. This is probably the earliest evidence of the impact of our native language on our vocalizations – and it is the musical features of communication that are the first to develop.[6]

Music, Williams demonstrates, affects and informs our development from our earliest beginnings right through to adulthood, but has some of its most profound impact during the formative years of childhood and adolescence.

A child's world is even more musical than that of your average adult: young children still hear musical IDS [infant directed speech], may attend music groups that may or may not teach instruments, and general education often features music as well. Songs are used to teach social etiquette and community values, as well as maths, languages and physical education. On top of this children's television is crammed full of music that children seem to love but which often drives adults crazy.[7]

The impact of this stimulus varies depending on the degree to which children engage with music. Those who actively learn instruments or participate in musical activity including infant and toddler music and movement groups, benefit from its ability to facilitate a range of cognitive, motor and social skills, others simply respond and exist in a world that is more alive and attuned to the presence of music. In adolescence the importance of music seems to reach its psychological zenith:

In this period of life we first start to regularly use music as a tonic, a kind of self-medication. We learn about the music that makes us feel good and the music that makes us feel terrible, and we begin to experiment with emotion through music. Music also mirrors and perhaps even helps to shape the development of our personal and social identity. Through these and other processes ... the music of this unique period becomes heavy with nostalgia and, as a consequence, is thought by many people to be the very best music of their life.

Music in our teenage years helps to shape identity, forming the basis for ideas that remain with us throughout life.

Both Campbell and Williams remind us of the centrality of music and 'musicking' to childhood and adolescence. As Blacking suggests we all possess our own childhood musical culture that plays a pivotal role in our understanding of ourselves, and the world around us. No wonder, then, that music plays such a central role in theatre made for, by and with children and young people, in fact it is hard to conceive of a piece of performance made for this audience that would not include music in some way. For makers of children's theatre the presence of live music-making and the integration of instruments plays a central role in their processes and aesthetics.

Actor-musicianship and theatre for young audiences

As demonstrated in Chapter 1, some of the earliest examples of actor-musicianship in the UK have been in work directed at children and young people. Here the theatre director and internationally renowned expert in theatre for young audiences (TYA) Tony Graham offers his explanation of their presence:

From its earliest days, live music and sound have been integral to theatre for young audiences. It was Natalia Sats, the founder of Moscow's Bluebird Theatre for Children, who suggested to Sergei Prokofiev that he write a piece to introduce orchestral instruments to children. In the UK, the need for actor-musicians, like actor-teachers or actor-writers, grew out of the tightly-bound ensemble nature of the work. Small touring companies, often tied to regional repertory theatres, formed the backbone of this new movement in the 1960s and beyond. Performing in schools, community halls and similar kinds of non-theatrical venues, it was necessary to think beyond the orchestra pit. How much equipment could be packed into a touring van? It was, therefore, useful to work with portable musical instruments like violins, woodwind, keyboards and, often, a range of percussion that might be found in any school music department. The development of the electronic keyboard in the 1970s opened up a whole new world of sound to the touring theatre company …

Whereas secondary age drama, leaning towards social and political issues, focused more on the word, the text, and the play, primary school children and their teachers were more susceptible to the total theatre experience. This meant that design and sound and movement played a bigger role. Younger children were, in the course of their school day, more likely to sing, dance, paint, make and move than older pupils. For younger children, a theatre group with singers and players was an extension of the artistic continuum. The course of progressive education in the twentieth century is bound up with the ways in which pupils could experience and participate in live art and music.

One of my favourite theatre images involving musical instruments came about during rehearsals for *Jemima Puddle-Duck and her Friends* by Adrian Mitchell with music by Stephen McNeff. We couldn't find a convincing way for Mrs Snail to move slowly with her small house across the stage. I suggested that she swing her accordion on her back and start to crawl. Problem solved. Similarly, I recall, in another show, how a violin player made the creaking sound of a door opening in a spooky house. He then continued his bow action beyond the violin, in a slow, wide sweeping gesture in front of him, to represent the door being opened. Finding the image in the music and the instrument itself lifts the actor-musician (not to mention the audience) into another realm.

Tony Graham's contribution to this chapter is a reminder of just how central actor-musicianship has been to the development of TYA. European TYA is full of examples of companies that exploit actor-musicianship in their practice and in America too there are countless examples of companies who use music as an integrated element of their storytelling for children and young people. One company with a 30-year history in the UK, who are also creating interest in the US, are Oily Cart, who specialize in theatre for the very young and those with complex learning disabilities. In 2014 they added to their international portfolio of work by helping to develop the Lincoln Centre's education department's approach to autistic children in the New York area, in association with Jonathon Schmidt, associate artist of Manhattan's influential New Victory children's theatre and Artistic Director of the innovative TYA company Trusty Sidekick. In their work one can witness the varied ways in which actor-musicianship can be used to make 'music that is theatre and, indeed, theatre that is music',[8] as founding member of Oily Cart and its resident composer and MD Max Reinhardt puts it.

Oily Cart as case study

An examination of the use of actor-musicianship and live instruments in the performance work of Oily Cart is worthy of a full chapter, if not an entire book in itself; however, for the purposes of this enquiry I thought it useful to offer a brief look at the various ways in which the company have utilized instruments and music as an integrated part of their work. Their approach is by no means definitive, but it resonates well with some of the earlier observations that have been made about the process of directing and working with actor-musicians and is informed at its core by a very open approach to the use and inclusion of music-making. The company has been consistently run by its three founding members, Tim Webb, Claire de Loon and Max

Reinhardt, for some thirty years. They have between them developed an extraordinary ability to work in response to their unique and often 'impossible' audiences, which have included babies and children with profound and multiple learning disabilities, and to the talents and make-up of their casts, that often consist of a mixture of performers from varying backgrounds, both musical and otherwise. Although their pieces are mostly scripted by Tim Webb, they are created out of extensive development phases that often involve working exhaustively with materials, sounds and other stimulus; part of their multi-sensory approach to theatre making. Music is an integral part of this process, with much of it discovered and created as part of the rehearsal process or in response to their audience. As we have already identified, this approach is particularly sympathetic to the working methodologies of the actor-musician, who in turn provide the company with a musical framing that is responsive to the ebb and flow of their varied audiences.

Reinhardt, who was himself an actor-musician, began to move away from performance work as the company developed through the 1980s, eventually fulfilling the role of MD and composer. This ushered in a phase in the company's history when they would cast actor-musicians who were able to respond and react to their audiences in the way that Webb and Reinhardt had themselves when performing. As the company grew in artistic scope and vision and as Reinhardt's other career as a World Music expert and DJ began, so the company started to enlist the use of specialist musicians. These musicians were from the widest of musical backgrounds from internationally renowned jazz cellist Ernst Reijsiger, who created the musical landscape for their 2006 foray into 'baby theatre' *Baby Balloon*, through to Sierra Leonean percussionist George Panda, who became an Oily regular on shows including *Drum, Ring a Ding Ding* and *Tube.* What is significant about these collaborations is that the fluidity of their performance style, and the need for very intense interaction with their audiences, resulted in an extension of the performative dimensions of actor-musicianship. Even when their role was primarily as musician, the Oily Cart instrumentalists were and are part of the action. The multi-sensory nature of the work and the particular needs of their audiences means that, as Reinhardt suggests, the music is theatre and the theatre is music. *Ring a Ding Ding*, for example, saw George Panda riding around on a specially constructed tricycle that contained a range of bespoke and magical percussion instruments built by long-term Oily collaborator and instrument maker/inventor Jamie Linwood. Panda's main contribution to the show was musical, but it was impossible to divorce this sound from its physical presence, both in terms of the kinetic impact of the tricycle, but also Panda's own mesmeric presence as a performer and human being. Panda may be a musician first and foremost, but in Oily Cart shows he is part of the fabric of the action and very much a character within it. This act of musician-actorship if we can call it this, is replicated in most of their work. Perhaps we can end this section with examples from some of the most moving and powerful elements of their performance work.

In their shows for children with profound and multiple learning disabilities (PMLD) and those with Autistic Spectrum Disorder (ASD), the company have developed a way of engaging each individual in their audience regardless of the level of their disability. These shows are typically performed to very small audiences of less than ten, plus their carers, teachers or parents. Each show ends with what have become known as 'name songs'. The company gather around each audience member in turn, and sing an improvised song which contains only the child's name as its lyrical content. The focus is intensively on that individual and the performance guided by their particular needs and responses. The work requires a level of reciprocity that can only be achieved by live music-making and whether provided by specialist musician or cast member, the musical content is supremely sensitive and responsive to the moment. The results are breathtakingly beautiful and profoundly moving. For that moment the child becomes the centre of their own theatrical world: their name is the only word uttered or sung, forming the structure and fabric of the music; their needs and responses become the driver behind its performance and tone. Musical sound and the physical presence of the instrument becomes central to this relationship, the performers using everything at their disposal to reach out and engage their audience of one. This is perhaps the quintessential act of actor-musicianship: music-making becomes the mode and medium of the performance and the impact is always immediate and tangible. A wonderful example can be seen on YouTube clips of their 2006 ASD show *Blue*, but I would like to close this section by sharing this extraordinary example of the power of actor-musicians used in this way, from a recent training event that I initiated in collaboration with Oily Cart and Wyvern School for children with special needs in Ashford in the South East of England. A group of performers, including Canadian actor-musician and writer Amanda West Lewis, were working with a young PMLD group that included a girl with a particularly debilitating and life-limiting condition. The girl was in the late stages of the disease and although still attending the school she was spending most of the time lying down; her eyes closed, locked-off from the rest of the class, her teachers and family. The group were working on name songs as part of the performance training and they began performing to the girl as part of their work. The intensive nature of the multi-sensory experience and the presence and responsiveness of the live music-making connected with the girl and as her teachers and carers looked on, her eyes opened, her facial muscles began to respond and she experienced what will be one of the few moments of engagement with others and the world around her that she will have. I have certainly never experienced a moment that so powerfully illustrates the unique power and visceral impact of actor-musicianship.

The centrality of actor-musicianship and the integration of live music-making in performance, are clear in the work of Oily Cart and common to much work seen in the TYA sector. The child audience offers a window to the latent adult fascination with the very immediate impact of live music-making, one that is reminiscent of the very earliest use of multi-skilled performers in the work of Joan Littlewood and the early Bubble companies. Both aim to engage new audiences:

for the Bubble and Littlewood this was defined by social demographic or class; for the TYA movement it is defined by age and need. The same could also be argued for the success of the more recent mainstream actor-musician shows such as *Once* and *Sweeney Todd*. In many ways they satisfy a need for reinvention, a chance to engage a new audience with older ideas. John Doyle's reworkings of extant musicals allow the material to be owned by a new generation, by the audience of the here and now; *Once* in turn offers a fresh approach to contemporary musical theatre, and allows the aesthetic of pop and folk music to find its way into the grand spaces of the West End, Broadway and beyond. They could all be seen in this sense as 'young theatre'.

Beatboxing as actor-musicianship

For Joan Littlewood, Glen Walford and John MacGrath the integration of music was a necessary constituent in any performance work that sought to break with the elitism associated with the theatre of the mid-to-late twentieth century. Their vision in this sense shares much with the German theatre makers pioneering a '*Junges Theater*'. This same impulse can be found in the ideas and ethos that governs the powerful hip-hop movement that has had such a significant impact on youth culture in America, Western Europe and much of the world.

Hip-hop is underpinned by a strong political and cultural identity that is interwoven with its history as an Afro-American art form. It is built on what are frequently described as its four pillars: break dance, DJing, graffiti art and MCing or rapping. Closely aligned to this aesthetic is the need to make work that is achievable by and aimed at others who identify with the so-called 'hip-hop generation'. With a history that stretches back to the 1980s, this 'hip-hop generation' can be quite widely defined and includes artists in their 40s and 50s. Nonetheless, the movement can be seen largely as being identified as a part of youth culture. It has a radical and political dimension, seeking to represent and reflect those from working-class backgrounds or who have experienced deprivation or social exclusion at the hands of the predominantly white mainstream holders of power. It can no longer be identified solely as a black cultural movement, but one that embraces all creeds and colours. Fundamental to the hip-hop aesthetic, however, and perhaps most pertinent to our enquiry, is its reliance on interdisciplinarity and its embracing of music as an integrated element of performance. On every street corner and in most school yards it seems, you can now find a rapper accompanied by a beatboxer, who creates a live accompaniment of vocalized drum sounds, sung elements and an impressive repertoire of musical sound. The modern beatboxer uses technology, such as looping and processors, to extent their range, often allowing them to create entire musical textures and layered patterns of sounds, giving birth to a new breed of musical performer who can generate whole sound-scapes from their own mouths. It is here in the beatboxer that we perhaps meet the most recent incarnation of actor-musicianship. The instrument has been absorbed into the body of the performer, but the means of expression remains the same; the act of music-making is integrated into the act of performance. The expression is vocal and musical, not singing, but a hybrid musical expression much closer to the act of playing an instrument. The music cannot be divorced from the act of performance, with most beatboxers extending their sonic output into the physical, with hand-gesture and movement that supports and extends its impact. One can also find elements of actor-musicianship in DJing and rapping. The DJ's physical presence is engaging and alive. They are part of the action of the event, often the star, somewhere between rock-star-singer and musician, with physi-cality informed by the act of spinning, scratching and changing records or digital musical material. They reshape their music in response to the moment, the needs of the crowd or the narrative of the rapper, often providing musical punctuation and illustration, in the same way a musical score might support a dramatic narrative. The rapper too shares some of the core characteristics of actor-musicianship. They are both singer and instrumentalist. Like the beat-boxer, they exist in a performative space somewhere between musical expression and speech. The text is paramount, but its meaning is deeply informed by its musical shape and timbre. There is much in the hip-hop aesthetic that is reminiscent of actor-musicianship and a lot in the act of performance that could be read as such.

In the development of hip-hop theatre we also see the potential for the continuation and development of actor-musicianship. Danny Hoch, the founder of New York's Hip Hop Theatre Festival defines the brief history of hip-hop theatre in this extract from his 2006 article *Here We Go, Yo ... A manifesto for a new hip-hop arts movement.*[9]

In the past 10 years, a new wave of hip-hop arts has taken shape in the form of dance, music, writing, visual art and theatre. These new works follow hip-hop's aesthetics closely, and yet they are not wholly comprised of graffiti art, breakdancing, DJ-sampling or rap. These works are products of a generation that grew up as hip-hoppers and is now branching out of the fundamentalist hip-hop book of elements and rules. Some works are created by traditional hip-hop artists who feel limited by the original four elements, yet wish to continue the aesthetic; some are made by hip-hop kids who went to art school, others by art school kids who discovered hip-hop later in life. Some of the creators are old-school B'boys (breakdancers) who have recognized that, as artists, they want to do more than perform in Las Vegas as an 'attraction'. Others are old-school graffiti artists whose gallery work has provided a vastly different context for their vision of what they can do with paint (or with other materials-many hip-hop clothing designers are ex-graffiti artists). Still others are rappers who feel the need to expand the possibilities of their storytelling beyond the 16 bars they are allotted on a record. For me hip-hop theatre provides the best paradigm for examining what the new hip-hop aesthetics are, what they aren't and what they could be.

Hip-hop theatre is a 'young theatre'. It is a theatre, as Hoch defines, that seeks to be made '*by, about* and *for* the hip-hop generation, participants in hip-hop culture or both'.[10] It can be found in many countries across the world and often includes the integration of music-making and the use of actor-musicianship in the form of beatboxing and human generated music-making as either an element or in some cases the core performative dimension. Berlin's Theater Strahl's TYA mask show *Klasse Klasse* is a collaboration between the company and German beatbox champion Daniel Mandolini, known as Mando. The piece describes itself as 'beatbox theatre' and as this review in the *Berlin Morgenpost* suggests, it is the integration of the beatboxing that accounts for much of its impact on its audience:

> Visually and musically this is probably the coolest theatre production for young people over 12 anywhere in Berlin … he [Mando] trans-forms a room full of noisy teenagers into a mesmerized audience listening in breathless fascination.[11]

In the UK beatboxer Shlomo has been creating his own version of 'beatbox theatre' with a series of projects that have performed across the country and perhaps most notably at the Purcell Rooms, part of London's Royal Festival Hall, a venue with a reputation for hybrid music-theatre events. His 2010 project *The Vocal Orchestra* produced a piece they called *Boxed,* the first to label itself 'beatbox theatre', which the publicity described as 'beatboxing's answer to *Stomp*, the Blue Man Group and *Into the Hoods*'[12]. There then followed a series of theatre pieces that included *Human Geek Box*, a one-man show that toured the UK, and a notable collaboration with classical ballet, which saw Shlomo performing on stage with fellow beatboxer Reeps One and dancers from the English National Ballet in the interdisciplinary dance-theatre piece *Ballet Meets Beatbox.* In America too there are examples of beatboxing as an integrated element of performance including *Bomb-itty of Errors,* a production based on Shakespeare's *Comedy of Errors* that came out of New

York City before touring internationally. Washington's Smithsonian even included a beatboxing storyteller in its family offerings as part of the 2014 Discovery Theater programme. Multi-talented performer Christylez Bacon was listed as follows in the theatre's publicity:

> He multi-tasks between various instruments such as the West African djembe drum, acoustic guitar and human beat-box ... all while continuing the oral tradition of storytelling from his life and heart.[13]

Hip-hop theatre, sharing as it does so many of the impulses and ideals that prompted the earlier pioneers of actor-musicianship in the UK, appears to be signalling one direction of travel for this practice as it is embraced by this most musical of generations. Integrating and making music is only one component of a youth arts culture that seems to embrace interdisciplinarity. A 'young theatre' is a multi-sensory theatre it seems and one that has to fight for its place as a live art form, against the tide and dominance of recorded media, film and television.

'Liveness' as an argument for actor-musicianship

Actor-musicianship is a live art form, its visceral appeal to audiences is dependent on the particular thrill of watching someone play an instrument, right there in front of their very eyes and ears. In this sense it taps into arguments and ideas around 'liveness' in performance. In the second edition of his book *Liveness: Performance in a Mediatized Culture,* Philip Auslander confesses to being surprised by the continued important of liveness within music consumption. In early editions he pointed to the controversy that surrounded the 1980s pop group Milli Vanilli, who were famously outed as having lip-synced to their own records. This was seen as a betrayal to music fans, a form of deceit. With so much mechanized music now on offer it would seem that interest in liveness in music might be irrelevant, but as Auslander remarks this does not seem to be the case. He cites the Ashlee Simpson scandal of 2004,[14] but there are other more recent events such as Beyonce at the inauguration of Obama and Dolly Parton at Glastonbury Festival in 2014, which demonstrate a continued interest in the liveness of music-making. In both cases there is little doubting the ability of these artists as singers and live-performers, but still it seems when we watch music-makers we wish them to be authentic; to be really playing right there in front of us. In a recent forum discussion I held on actor-musicianship at London's Bargehouse on the South Bank, actor-musician and member of the original West End company of *Return to the Forbidden Planet* Ben Fox remarked on the particular thrill and power of live music-making even when it is depicted on television and film. In the UK and US there are now very few TV programmes that actually screen live music performances, preferring instead to fall back on the relative safety and stability of miming or working to backing tracks. Those rare shows that honour the liveness of music, such as Jools Holland's BBC Two series *Later With Jools Holland* or the broadcasts from the Grand Ole Opry in the US, attract a very particular excitement and engagement from their audiences. It seems, as Auslander suggests, that liveness is still important.

If theatre is to fight its corner and survive in this age of computer gaming, television, film and video streaming, then one of its strongest suits has to be its liveness. The experience of watching real people interact, and indeed the thrill of engaging in work that is responsive to the moment and its audience, has to be part of its unique appeal and at least an element in its continued survival and relevance. Actor-musicianship is perhaps one of the livest examples of liveness in theatre; surely its continuation and the current upsurge in its appeal has to be bound up in this fact. Whether watching *Sweeney Todd* in a theatre with hundreds of others, or having a name song sung to you alone, the visceral and phenomenological impact of actor-musicianship has to be part of its success in this world of vicarious, prerecorded engagement with story and performance. The *Guardian* critic Lyn Gardner argues that only theatre that engages its audience in an act of interaction will survive in our mediatized world.[15] Actor-musicians and live music-making offer us that opportunity and although there are many arguments for the survival of theatre, perhaps one of the most powerful for the development of actor-musicianship can be found in its liveness. Let us close the book then with this warning of sorts from Gardner, which appeared in her 2006 review of Oily Cart's extraordinary ASD show *Blue:*

> This is not a theatrical experience that you watch, but one that you all share. Other contemporary theatre-makers should take note.[16]

Notes

1 Taube, G. *Young Theatre in Germany: Contemporary Theatre for Children and Young People* published in "IXYPSILONZETT" *Magazine for Children's and Young People's Theatre*, No. 1, 2008. English translation available: http://www.jugendtheater.net/fileadmin/inhalt/themen/pdf/xyz08engl_taube.pdf (accessed 8 January 2015).

2 Blacking, J., *How Musical Is Man?* (Seattle: University of Washington Press, 1973).

3 Shehan Campbell, P., *Songs in their Heads* (New York: Oxford University Press, 2010).

4 Small, C., *Musicking: The Meanings of Performing and Listening* (Hanover, NH: Wesleyan University Press, 1998; cited in Campell 2010), ibid.

5 Williamson, V., *You Are the Music: How Music Reveals what it Means to be Human.* (London: Icon Books, 2014).

6 Williamson, V., ibid., 22

7 Williamson, V., ibid., 32

8 Brown, M., ed., *Oily Cart: All Sorts of Theatre for all Sorts of Kids* (London: Institute of Educaton Press, Trentham Books, 2012), 41.

9 Hoch, D. (2006) *Here We Go, Yo … A manifesto for a new hip-hop arts manifesto* The Theatre Communications Group: http://www.tcg.org/publications/at/dec04/go.cfm (accessed 9 January 2015).

10 Hoch, D., *Here We Go, Yo …*, ibid.

11 *Berliner Morgenpost* as cited on Theater Strahl's own publicity for *Klasse Klasse*: www.theater-strahl.de (accessed 7 January 2015).

12 South Bank Centre's publicity for *Boxed* January 2010.

13 Publicity for July 2014 run at Discovery Theater of Christylez Bacon show for children five–16 years of age: The Smithsonian Associates website (accessed 6 January 2015).

14 Auslander, P., *Liveness: Performance in a Mediatized Culture*, 2nd edn (Abingdon: Oxon, Routledge, 2008), xi.

15 Gardner, L. *Wisdom of the Crowd: Interactive Theatre is Where it is at*, *The Guardian* Theatre Blog, Tuesday 2 March 2010: http://www.theguardian.com/stage/theatreblog/2010/feb/28/interactive-theatre-connected-coney-lift (accessed 9 January 2015).

16 Gardner, L. review of *Blue* for *The Guardian*, 5 July 2006.